CHRISTMAS PAST
A selection from Victorian Magazines

CHRISTMAS PAST

A selection from Victorian Magazines
compiled by

Dulcie M. Ashdown

Foreword by Jilly Cooper

A MERRY CHRISTMAS & A HAPPY NEW YEAR

A HUNDRED THOUSAND WELCOMES

BOOK CLUB ASSOCIATES
LONDON

This edition published 1977 by
Book Club Associates
By arrangement with Elm Tree Books

Copyright © 1976 by Dulcie M. Ashdown

Printed in Great Britain by
Ebenezer Baylis & Son Ltd
The Trinity Press, Worcester, and London

Foreword

IT IS OFTEN SAID that the Victorians invented Christmas as we know it today. But I think what is meant by this is that the Victorians pinned down the commercial opportunities, and swung into action to create what is now perhaps little more than a great consumer festival. After all they did invent Christmas cards (described in this book as the 'little artistic works with which our home is flooded at the festive time'). And they certainly found the story of the working-class Jewish boy born in a shed in the stony Judean hills too spartan and unromantic and wrapped it up in tinsel with heavenly babes, candle-lit Christmas trees, presents, turkey and plum pudding. Victorian lady poets even changed the weather, waxing lyrical about the 'bleak mid-winter,' and 'snow on snow' when the average December temperature in Israel is about 80 degrees in the shade.

It is to the Victorians, too, that we are indebted for the arrival of that red-cheeked senile old braggart Father Christmas, although I think they would be appalled by the 20th-century Santa Claus in a big department store who when recently asked why he was wearing shin pads under his red robes replied: 'Well if the little sods asked for something last year and they didn't get it, they come back this year and kick the hell out of me.'

Christmas of course is essentially a children's festival and perhaps only looked forward to with excitement by children. My husband says it was the only time he saw his family united and happy. Nowadays as adults we tend to regard it as nothing more than a chance to catch up on some sleep and watch the country grind to a halt, not to mention the trauma of deciding with whose family the holiday will be spent.

But I do remember the Christmases of my childhood so well. They were essentially Victorian, which was hardly surprising for both my parents were brought up by families firmly ensconced in the Victorian era. There was the mounting excitement as the Christmas tree was delivered, the walks to gather wild holly to decorate the house, the mysterious parcels delivered to the door by post, and the mounting ranks of Christmas cards from all those friends and relations one managed to forget about for the rest of the year.

And in this charming book, it is the descriptions of things to do at Christmas that bring the memories flooding back: the fancy dress parties with all the excitement of my mother finishing my costume just in time, the dumb crambo, the blind man's bluff, the charades – although some of the games recommended strike me as being rather hazardous. There is one that involves pouring brandy over a bowl of fruit, setting light to it, and then asking people to plunge their hands through the flames to 'obtain possession of the fruit.'

Or even more dangerous is the game in which a candle was lighted and placed on a table, the player blind-folded, turned round several times and then dispatched to blow out the candle – resulting, one would have thought, in an awful lot of singed eyelashes.

One thing that amazes me is how much they ate in those days – enough to make a calorie-counter's hair stand on end. And how cheap it all was. One's mouth waters as one reads details of a family Christmas dinner costing £1.13s.1d., which included celery soup, cod with garlic-flavoured sauce, boiled turkey, quails, roast beef, Ox tongue à la Belgravia, Christmas pudding, mince pies, and orange sponge jelly.

With typical Victorian thrift they were also very good with left-overs; anyone struggling to make ends meet today can find recipes for 'pea soup out of yesterday's bones,' or 'fricassie of hare from yesterday's soup.' Although I didn't like the sound of fowl sandwiches.

The advice on giving presents is absolute heaven, too. 'It would be certainly difficult,' says one contributor, 'to find a more welcome gift than some trifle bought at the Parisian Diamond Company in Regent Street . . . For a classical head, what could be prettier than a bandeau of diamonds?' What indeed.

'There are diamond buckles galore,' she goes on, 'and we cannot exist without a Louis XVI buckle in these days any more than we can a dangle.' A 'dangle' turns out rather disappointingly to be a 'lucky diamond pig' with ruby eyes.

The writer then moves on to a section entitled Whiffs from the South of France, which makes one think of garlic and Gauloises, but turns out to be scent. 'It is a recognised fact that one scent a man is not ashamed to use is lavender.' A far cry from the battalion of bottles on Harrods' aftershave counter today.

But if you couldn't afford diamonds or lavender, you would have found some very bizarre suggestions for presents you could run up yourself, much in the Woman's Own Crochet-Your-Own-Royal-Family vein. Imagine the difficulty of convincingly saying: 'Just what I wanted' when you were presented with a 'picture easel made from the lid of a disused box', or a 'slipper-shaped holder for a feather broom', or even worse a cornet made of cardboard lined with crimson satin and covered with silk to be hung 'from a projecting bracket near an invalid's bed to hold a cup of water or a case of flowers'. I'd much rather have a dangle.

As there was no television or wireless in those days, people either read or were read to or told ghost stories. This was also the time when the first women's magazines appeared, and the concept of the serial was born. The Victorian middle classes, newly spewed up by the Industrial Revolution, had of course created a world in which they needed guidance on how to behave, and they relied largely on the advice and lifestyles offered by magazine stories. Some of the most fascinating and hilarious extracts in Christmas Past are taken from contemporary fiction. Certainly every wither is wrung as stingy, self-important church wardens see the error of their ways, and drunks reform, and careworn wives grow brighter and stronger, and little girls become the apples of their crusty old grandfathers' eyes.

There can scarcely have been a dry eye when readers finished the story about the doctor dying of poverty, who addressed his last words to his dog:

'Ye never heard o' God, Skye, or the Saviour, for ye're just a puir doggie . . . but ye're a bonnie beastie Skye, ye've been true and kind to your master Skye and ye'll miss him if he leaves ye. Some day ye'll die also, and they'll bury ye, and I doubt that'll be the end o' ye, Skye.'

Nor do the Victorians sidestep the sterner issues; there's a splendidly moral tale about suspected adultery during Christmas week, in which a husband tries to drown his wife. The author is called Headon Hill, and he allows the jealous husband to go through every torment before he ends up sobbing thankfully at his sleeping wife's bedside as the Christmas bells peal out.

Then there is the rousing tale of the English family staying in a Dutch château for the shooting. They are beseiged by a crowd of licentious Belgian soldiery, and the mother and children hide in the attic.

'And if they shoot papa?', asks one of the children.

' "If they hurt a hair of his head, all England would come to chop Belgium and Holland to mincemeat," said I, choosing a Christmas simile; "for Papa has been an English Dragoon Captain." '

One laughs, but a little wistfully, as one remembers a time when Britain really did rule the waves, and such jingoism was possible. Equally as one giggles at Victorian sentimentality and sanctimoniousness, one cannot help envying their gilt-edged security and confidence.

What really impresses me, however, is the saintliness of the children, with their rosy cheeks, and eternally sparkling eyes (it must have been the reflection of all those dangles), as they spend all their saved-up pocket money on buying a Christmas dinner for the impoverished.

'It's about the little Carsons, Philip,' begins one story. 'If you only knew what a hole they live in.'

And finally ends when they return tired from their errand of mercy:

'I say, old girl,' said Philip, 'I don't think I ever had such a happy day in my life.'

'I don't know what we should have done without your six shillings, Phil.'

'I say, Maggie.'

'Well old fellow.'

'Let's do it again.'

Perhaps if I'd brought up my own children more strictly they might have harboured more altruistic feelings towards their fellow men, but alas a leopard can't change his Spock.

I took my son to a Christmas service last year in aid of Shelter. During the service, he sat bootfaced while we had prayers for the Homeless, hymns for the Homeless, and finally a long sermon about the homeless. This was followed by a collection. As I was situated near the headmistress, I felt I ought to put in a £1 note.

My son looked positively thunderous. 'What's the matter?' I said on the way home. 'Why do you waste a whole £1,' he said furiously, 'just to help the hopeless?'

Jilly Cooper

Compiler's Note

THE VICTORIAN CHRISTMAS is everyone's ideal of what a Christmas ought to be: children enraptured before a candle-lit tree, tables groaning under an abundance of turkey, goose and pudding, carol-singers with bright lanterns in shining snow, church bells ringing through midnight air. Those Victorian Christmases which Charles Dickens depicted have passed into the canon of our most cherished literature, and have become as much a part of our ideal of the festive season as the nostalgia of our own childhood memories. It is surely no accident that Victorian scenes are among the most popular pictures on our modern Christmas cards.

Looking further back in time, we may remember the Yule logs, the mummers and the roasted sides of beef which featured in the baronial halls of the Middle Ages, but it is only in the last hundred years or so that Christmas feasts and entertainments have been shared by the majority, rather than by the privileged few. As improving social conditions brought the middle and 'working' classes a measure of prosperity, the celebrations enjoyed by the aristocracy and the wealthy had their imitations in suburban villa, country cottage and slum tenement alike. 'Christmas as at Windsor' came to be the established order, for it was the festivities of the royal family that the Victorians took as their model. The German customs brought by Prince Albert into Queen Victoria's ever-expanding nursery were, paradoxically, the basis of the typically English Christmas which we claim today, and had, by the time of his death in 1861, begun to be adopted by the doting *pater familias* throughout the land.

The popular Press was mainly responsible, of course, for the wide dissemination of the new ideas, as magazines directed to men or women, old or young, were finding a new mass market. From the middle of the 1860s, Christmas features, stories, poems and pictures, beyond the purely religious sphere, won a place in December issues. Just because they could read Dickens's newly-minted stories of Mr Pickwick's jovial doings at Dingley Dell, or of the Cratchetts' feast at the gift of the converted Scrooge, the Victorians did not lose their taste for lesser fiction on seasonal themes. They thrilled to tales of ghosts and hob-goblins, wept at pictures of orphans in the snow and revelled in a good love-story in a Christmas setting.

In spanning some forty years of Victorian Christmases, from the magazines read by the Victorians themselves, a picture emerges of the security and confidence in which they rejoiced. Their meals, their clothes, their home-made entertainments and gifts – even their self-conscious remembrance of charity and the claims of the poor in the midst of their own indulgence – come to us fresh from the pages of the Victorians' own reading-matter. They come to us fresh, but they are also familiar, for their Christmas customs have become our traditions. As we try to recreate the season of good-will and merriment, we give new life to our own ideal of 'Christmas past'.

Dulcie M. Ashdown

No. 36. December 1st, 1868.   Registered for Transmission Abroad.   Price One Penny.

THE INFANT'S MAGAZINE.

CHRISTMAS PUDDING.

WHEN merry, frosty Christmas comes,
Mamma takes currants, peel, and plums;
Spice, raisins, flour, and eggs she takes,
And with them all a pudding makes;
So we are glad when Christmas comes
And brings us puddings full of plums.

CHRISTMAS CAKE.

When round the table we all sit
Papa gives each of us a bit,
And baby, too, must have a slice,
Because it is both sweet and nice.

CHRISTMAS GIFTS.

CHRISTMAS has come, with gifts and toys,
For little girls as well as boys.
Mary has got a picture-book,
At which she and her sisters look;
And Jane has got a gilded fan,
And something nice has come for Ann;
Baby has got a neat doll, drest
In scarlet coat and bright blue vest—
Mary and Jane, and Ann I know,
When Christmas comes with frost & snow,
Will think upon the girls and boys
Who get no pretty Christmas toys
Who suffer want, and cold, and care,
And help them, both by alms and prayer.

Little

DECEMBER, 1877.

FRONTISPIECE—"Unequal Odds."

☞ TO OUR READERS.—For Notice as to EXHIBITION of "LITTLE FOLKS" WORK, see January Part.

Folks

CASSELL PETTER & GALPIN: LONDON, PARIS & NEW YORK.

THE STORY OF A CHRISTMAS-TREE.

CHAPTER I.

"I SAY, Philip!"

"Get out of my way, Maggie. You're treading on the tail of my kite!"

"I beg your pardon; I am very clumsy; but, Philip, I have a scheme."

"Oh, well, that's nothing new, you're always having schemes. Get away, can't you; girls are always coming where they are not wanted."

The tears stood in Maggie's eyes, but still she lingered a minute.

"It's about those little Carsons. Oh, Philip, if you only knew what a hole they lived in, you wouldn't be so cross with me!"

Philip failed entirely to see the logical connection between the two ideas; but Maggie very rarely cried, and at the sight of coming tears he relented. So pushing back his cap, he looked up from the kite he was mending to say, rather sharply, "Well, what's the bother now?"

The two children were playing in an outhouse adjoining the rectory, and they made a fine contrast as they stood there for a moment looking into one another's eyes—Philip, with his head thrown a little back, and Maggie half turning towards the open door. They were both sunburnt, and roughly dressed, but Philip was thickset and black-eyed, while his sister was a slim little thing, with hair of that rich colour which the old artists painted for gold.

"Well, you see, it isn't so very long till Christmas," said Maggie, hesitatingly.

"Nearly three months," interrupted Philip.

"But we only get fourpence a week, and I was thinking if we could save up."

"Oh, good gracious, Maggie! I want to buy myself a paint-box—I must have one, in fact."

"Very well," said Maggie, with a little half-suppressed sigh. "Then I suppose I must manage it alone."

"I do wish you wouldn't make such mysteries, Maggie. What has all this to do with the Carsons?"

"Why, father went to see them yesterday, and he says that now the father and mother are dead, that little Milly does all the work, and starves herself to feed the rest."

"Why don't they go into the 'house?'" suggested Philip.

Maggie shuddered. "You haven't been into the town lately, Philip; you forget what the 'house' looks like. Besides, their father made them promise they wouldn't before he died."

"Did he!" said Philip, and with that he went on mending his kite.

Maggie had taken up her jacket from the bench in one corner, and was preparing to go.

"I thought," said Philip, "that they were being helped out of the poor-box."

"So they are," said Maggie, with a fierce flash out of her grey eyes. "And they've help from the parish too, if you want to know; but that isn't much for six children to live upon, and only Bob earning anything. And I think it's a shame, Philip, to talk as you do. If you'd like to live on bread-and-cheese and potatoes, as those poor things live, I'm much mistaken," and with that she swung out of the room, and banged the door, only opening it again for a moment to put her head inside, and shout out, "No butter, mind!"

CHAPTER II.

"FATHER," said Philip, a day or two after, "what are you doing to help those Carsons?"

Mr. Leighton looked down rather wistfully into the frank boyish face that was lifted so earnestly towards his own. Since his wife's death his children had been his constant care and delight, and he was not slow to discern their thoughts.

"I pay for the baby at the *crèche*, my boy, but that's all I can afford just now."

"Father, you know that you promised that if I would save up three shillings towards a paint-box, you would give me the other three?"

"Yes, dear."

"Well, should you mind if I used the six shillings for something else?"

Mr. Leighton glanced down at him sharply. "Please yourself, my boy."

"Thank you, father; how good you are!"

They were busy planting shrubs in the rectory

garden, while Maggie finished her French exercise in the schoolroom.

Presently Mr. Leighton called Philip's attention to a fine fir-tree. "I think this must be what you had for your Christmas-tree last year. By-the-by, perhaps you think you are growing too old for Christmas-trees; would you like to make some other use of it this year?"

"Might we carry it down to Milly Carson?"

"Do just what you like with it, Philip; I am not afraid to trust you or Maggie either."

CHAPTER III.

IT was a cold windy night in December, and Milly Carson sat darning socks by the light of a farthing dip. She shivered a little, for the fire was very low, and she had no more coal. The baby sister who had been at the *crèche* all day had come home for the night, and Milly was rocking the little wooden cradle with her foot. She was only fourteen, and very small for her age, but by this dim light she looked like an old woman. Her threadbare dress was neatly mended, and the room was scrupulously clean, but the supper set out on the deal table looked as if it would hardly have satis-

"MILLY CARSON SAT DARNING SOCKS."

fied one of the three hungry children who sat round it. Milly herself did not join in it, for there was Bob still to come, and she knew he would be hungry after his day's work. It was the day before Christmas Eve, and she could not help thinking of this time last year, when her father was alive. She remembered how he had come in with a heap of bright holly on his shoulder, and a pile of wood in his arms, his pockets full of groceries for the Christmas pudding, and his purse heavier than usual. With the holly they had made together what the children called "a tree," and covered it with bright flags, and oranges, and apples; the wood was to make a real Christmas fire; and the heavy purse had enabled Milly to choose little Christmas gifts for everybody next day. But this year the cupboard was empty, and the purse was empty too, and there was no father to come home and kiss them

all. Bob would bring eight shillings, but six were owing for rent, and the other two would have to go for bread and firing. She cried a little quietly to herself, for she had always meant to save enough to give the children their Christmas dinner; and then, just when her little earnings had reached the right amount, Bob had sprained his ankle and lost a week's work, so that her money-box had to be emptied. Bob had never been told the secret purpose for which this money had been intended, and now that he was able to go to work again he hoped in time to be able to replace it.

"There's Bob!" said little ten-year-old Esther, springing to the door. Louie, the next child, was a cripple, so she had to sit still in her high chair, but she had the first kiss from Bob, after all. Willie, who was Esther's special pet and plaything, looked up in the middle of his crust, to say—

"Tiss Esther too—see opened de door."

"Esther's always a handy little lass," said Bob, patting her on the head as he set down the loaf on the table.

Milly had brushed away the tears at the sound of her brother's step, and was now busy stirring the contents of a saucepan over the fire. "Come and warm thee hands, Bob," she said; and then in an undertone she added, "what about the rent?"

The boy, who was two years younger than Milly, threw up his cap with a laugh before he hung it on the peg. "Why, Milly?" he said, "my hands are as warm as hot buns, and the rent's all in the right place; but, I say, what do you think my master's been up to? Come, now, three guesses for you each."

"Oh, Bob!" said Milly, with a sudden scared look, "he hasn't been a-turning of you off, has he?"

Oh, how Bob did laugh! it did one good to hear him; and then all the little Carsons laughed, and finally Milly laughed too.

"P'raps he has given you another book?" said the little cripple; "I hope it's got pictures in it like the other."

"Try again," said Bob, as he sat down to his hot porridge.

THE ARRIVAL OF THE CHRISTMAS-TREE.

"Is it a pair o' boots?" suggested Esther.

"No; but I'll tell you what it is," said Bob, bringing down his spoon on to his plate with ringing emphasis. "It's a good ton o' first-rate coals; that's what it is, so there!" And certainly the most first-rate embers ever lighted could hardly have flashed more brightly than did Bob's eyes at that moment.

"Oh, Bob!" exclaimed the breathless Milly, "then there's one-and-six to spare, after all, for thou did not have to buy firing."

"I should think," said Louie, as her dreaming eyes watched the snowflakes come down outside, "God must have known it was going to be a cold night."

Esther now put her curly head close up to Bob's ear, and said, in a low whisper, "Could us get Willie a new cap?"

"Esther's dot no fings herself for Sundays," observed Willie.

"I was thinking about a Christmas pudding," Milly ventured to suggest.

Bob had given Esther a mild shove back into her place at table, and now he turned to Milly as the only one whose suggestion was worth answering. "Yes," he said, "that's just what I want to talk to you about. First of all, I thought I'd have a bit of a holly-tree for the children (Bob was just twelve), and then it seemed that was a silly notion, being as we'd scarce enough to eat; so I did think I'd get some stuff for a pudding, but I've changed my mind," and Bob folded his arms in a very decisive manner. The little ones were all watching him, and Milly looked up anxiously.

But still Bob was silent for a minute. Then he broke out in a half-combative way: "Look ye here, now; we *are* poor, I don't deny, but has there ever been a day when we hadn't bread to eat? I don't say as we've had milk every day, or taters every day, and lard of course is 'extry;' but I should like to know if there's ever been a day as we haven't had a crust of bread?"

"We used to have meat sometimes," said Esther.

"Now, look thee here, Esther," said Bob; "I wouldn't be greedy if I was thee. I've been hearing this night about them folk in India what's dropping down dead i' the street for want of bread and water. Yes," he continued, as the children turned towards him with horror-struck faces of pity and amazement, "Yes, Esther—dozens of them, men and women an' little babes—an' if they're not helped their country will be one big graveyard."

There was a solemn stillness in the room, and then little Louie said, "Let's give the money to them, Bob."

"Bless thee heart, Louie!" said Bob. "That's just what I was thinking, and that's why I didn't get the stuff for the pudding. The men in our shops clubbed together what they could spare, but I wouldn't give them our one-and-six till I'd asked you all at home, because, you see, it's yours."

"It's thy earnings," said Milly; "but it was kind to wait, and I do think the poor Indians want it the most."

"Hindoos, Milly, not Indians," said Bob.

"Sall I send 'em my top?" said Willie, at once bethinking himself of his greatest treasure.

Then there was a laugh; but Esther said, "Well, it was very kind of him, I'm sure! And Bob needn't have called me greedy, because I should like to send them the money as much as any of you." And when the children knelt down that night, they all prayed for the poor starving people, but they somehow forgot to ask anything for themselves. Only little Louie said softly, at the end of her prayer, "Please, God, I should so like Willie to have a new cap—some day."

CHAPTER IV.

AT about three o'clock in the afternoon of the following day Milly was startled by a loud rap. The snow was falling heavily, and she was rather startled when she opened the door, to see Maggie and Philip standing out in the cold with a heavily-laden market basket between them.

"Are the children all out?" Maggie asked, in an eager whisper.

"They're all at school, except Louie, miss, and she's reading to the blind old lady next door; would you please to step in, miss?"

"Thank you," said Maggie; and then she blushed and frowned, and said to her brother, "You explain."

Philip set down the basket inside the house, took off his cap and shut the door, and then said rather abruptly, "Please, don't be offended, but we should like to empty our basket."

Milly's brown eyes opened wonderingly. "Can I help you, sir?"

"I wish you would!" said Philip. "Just take this 'grub' off to the larder. Stay, I'll carry the meat myself; it's rather heavy. The groceries will do for you to take; we thought they'd come in for a plum pudding."

"Yes, they're all for you," said Maggie, with a bright smile. "Father sent the beef, and the apples and pears and potatoes are out of the garden; but Phil and I bought the groceries ourselves."

Philip turned crimson, and thrust his head into the cupboard.

As for Milly, she looked for a minute as if she were going to be shot, and then she burst out crying and laughing together.

"Oh dear, oh dear!" she said, "there must be some mistake; it can't be *all* for us. Why, we haven't had a real dinner with meat and pudding and everything since father died!"

"Look here, Milly," said Philip, "you must make haste and put the things away, for there's something else coming."

"There it is!" said Maggie, springing to the door. There stood the gardener with a beautiful fir-tree in his arms, and a box of tapers and reflectors in his pocket.

"If you don't much mind," said Philip, "I think you'd better not light up the tree till to-morrow night, because we want you to invite us to see it, and we're to dine with father to-night."

CHAPTER V.

WHEN the little Carsons came home from church the next morning they were puzzled beyond measure to see the table set for dinner, with knives and forks, and to smell various suspicious and delightful odours suggestive of important cooking.

"My dears," cried Milly, with a little scream of delight, "there's roast beef and plum pudding, and potatoes and apples, and——."

"Oh my!" screamed Esther, "she has been keeping all them things in the yard, and that's why we mightn't open the yard door."

"Is I to have a little taste too?" said Willie, "or is there only a little of it?"

"Thou shall have twenty tastes, my precious," said Milly. "There's more than we can eat in a day, I do believe."

"Do you think," said Louie, "we might send a little taste of the pudding to the blind lady?"

"Let's ask her in," said Bob. "But, I say, Milly, where did it all come from?"

"I'll dish up now," said Milly, "and you can all guess afterwards."

The secret was all explained at dinner-time, and when Philip and Maggie came to tea, no king or queen ever received a more adoring welcome, and certainly kings and queens have seldom felt so happy as they did.

When the tea-things were all cleared away Philip begged Bob and Esther and little Willie to run to the end of the street and post him a letter. Louie might stay, he said, on condition that she shut her eyes and stopped her ears. Then he and Maggie opened the back door and carried in the tree out of the yard, Milly helping them.

When the children came running in, and Louie was allowed to open her eyes, that little bare room became a veritable paradise. The blind lady had been allowed to stay, and Philip had rushed out before tea to fetch a favourite kitten expressly for her. The tree was radiantly beautiful, and covered with bright pretty things. There was a cap for Willie, a book for Louie, and a bright scarf for Esther. Best of all, there was a great-coat which Philip had outgrown, and which Mr. Leighton had offered him for Bob, besides a beautiful warm jacket which had once been Maggie's, and which just fitted Milly. As the tapers died out the children all sang a Christmas hymn, and when it was over Mrs. Gordon kissed them all and said good-night. "I think," she said, "the Lord Christ is glad to have his birthday kept so."

As Maggie and Philip were walking home in the starlight, Philip put his arm round his sister's neck and kissed her.

"I say, old girl," he said, "I don't think I ever had such a happy day in my life."

"I don't know what we should have done without your six shillings, Phil!"

"I say, Maggie."

"Well, old fellow?"

"Let's do it again."

A. M.

AT THE CANNON'S MOUTH.

HOME FOR THE HOLIDAYS.

WE mounted the coach in haste and glee
  When the winter day was dawning,
  And we dashed on our way up hill and
    down,
By frosty meadow and red lit town,
All boys were we, as merry and free
  As birds on a fair spring morning.

All merry and free, so you had said,
  And hearty, had you seen us !
Yet Phil and I sat head to head,
  And a shadow there was between us.
My way I lost in each class he crossed ;
  By ready wit he won.
Was I to blame that he reaped the fame
  Ere half my task was done ?

Up hill and down, away we dashed,
  Hearts bound and hearts aloof,
Till the sun on the old church steeple flashed,
  And we greeted the stork on the roof,
And the noisy ducks on the frozen pond,

And the laughing village maiden,
And the pompous beadle shaking his wand,
  And the children holly-laden.

And then we wound to the lonelier road,
  Nor speed nor whirl abating ;
At our song and our shout the rooks flew out,
  From the fir-trees calmly waiting.
And a sight I saw that pleased me well—
  My brothers and little sister Nell
All welcoming in the snowy place,
And above them sweet my mother's face.

Then quick with a tear to Phil I turned,
  And I wrung and wrung his willing hand ,
For him on earth no mother yearned,
  And his father roamed in a far-off land.
He answered me with his face aglow,
  For his was the finer feeling ;
But my own head felt like melted snow,
  And it seemed as if bells were pealing.

WINTER SPORTS.

JIM and Joe, away they go
To build a castle of the snow;
Snow so white the castle walls,
Snow so hard the cannon balls;
And peeping out above the hold,
A giant's head of snow so cold.
"Hallo!" said Jim, "when all is ready,
And tower and turret made quite steady,
We'll hoist a flag of
colours bright,
And then we'll have a
jolly fight;
We'll call the castle
Giant's Fort,
And get our friends to
join the sport.
Hugh, Nigel, Tom, my
soldiers three,
To keep the Giant's
Fort with me:
Whilst Ambrose, Nu-
gent, little Ben,
Walter, and Charles
shall be your men.
And little Bess, in
scarlet coat,
With comforter about her throat,
Shall be our Queen, and knight us when
We've shown that we are valiant men;
Walter shall bring her, and will see
That she shall safe from danger be.
But now our plans. First, you attack,
And we shall fight, and drive you
back;
A battle fought without a blow,
Our only weapons balls of snow.
To take the giant's head your aim;
Whilst to prevent it is our game.
To work! for well on either side

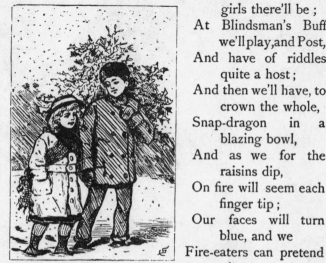

The troops with balls must be
supplied."
Said Joe, "It is a glorious plan.
I'll work as hard as e'er I can;
And when the battle's fought and
won,
We in the house will have some fun:
We'll ask the boys all home to tea,
And mother and the
girls there'll be;
At Blindsman's Buff
we'll play, and Post,
And have of riddles
quite a host;
And then we'll have, to
crown the whole,
Snap-dragon in a
blazing bowl,
And as we for the
raisins dip,
On fire will seem each
finger tip;
Our faces will turn
blue, and we
Fire-eaters can pretend
to be.
I know that mother will agree;
Our happiness she likes to see.
She says if we our lessons learn,
Some pleasure we deserve to earn,
And as we've worked and prizes won,
She's sure to help us in our fun."
Ah! winter is as full of joy
To every merry girl and boy,
As is the brighter summer day,
When they can in the meadow play;
Each season brings its own delight,
Or flowers so gay, or snow so
white.   J. G.

CHRISTMAS AND NEW YEAR PRESENTS.

AS I sit down to write this little paper on some easily - made presents, Christmas and the New Year are fast approaching.

There are few homes where they are not looked forward to as times of present, giving and receiving by old and young alike; for the old folks love to make the time a season of happiness to those around, that the young may some day look back on it as a bright memory never to be forgotten.

There are several merry ways and means of giving presents, and a few need but be mentioned to help many a bright-faced circle at once to set to work for the happy time. Christmas-trees we are all almost tired of, though they still delight very little folk. As every one knows how to decorate them, only three suggestions on that subject are necessary. Firstly, the trees look much more wintry and Christmas-like if new cotton wool is laid along the tops of their branches (always a difficult place to dress), to imitate snow; secondly, a snake cut out of a round piece of cardboard, and gilded, when carefully balanced on a large pin stuck into the very top of the tree, where the heat of the candles will make it revolve all the time, looks very well; thirdly, numbers of very small penny dolls (about two inches long), dressed in some very sparkling material, with shiny gauze wings, and hung about the dark parts of the tree, add wonderfully to its attractiveness.

A Christmas post-office is a merry-making in which all can join, from the oldest to the youngest, for even grandpapa and grandmamma like to get a Christmas letter. To do this, you must rail off with screens one large corner of the room where you intend to have it; these you can adorn with holly and other evergreens, one small opening being left, across which you put a little table. Hang up a cloth or shawl over the upper part, letting it come down just low enough to make a small square aperture, about the size of a railway ticket-office window. Behind this sits the post-mistress, and whoever goes to inquire for a letter is sure to get one addressed to them. In it they find a number, which, on showing at another large window (that should be made at the side of the office), is exchanged for a parcel bearing the same figure. Some people's correspondence is very large, and as many as thirteen or fourteen letters fall to the share of one person.

The amusement that is the prettiest way of giving presents is that of the period when Christmas was called "Yule-tide," and people burnt enormous Yule-logs, at which they roasted oxen and sheep whole; those may have been to a certain degree "the good old times," but they were undoubtedly very rough and uncomfortable when compared with our modern days. "Yule-traps" is, however, a part of the old customs that we may still keep up, as it gives great amusement. It consists in hiding one present in another, disguising it in such a manner as to test the cleverness of the receiver not a little in finding it out.

For example, a soft pair of kid gloves can be rolled up, and secured in a large Spanish walnut-shell previously emptied, and the two halves gummed together; a case of knitting-needles will be hidden in what appears to be nothing but a flat block of wood, which, by a little knowledge of simple carpentering can be made to slide into two pieces so as to discover it. A little pot of damson cheese has been found to have the preserve dexterously cut away underneath, sufficiently to give room for the pot to contain also a delicate gold chain or ornament. A large pair of swede turnips has been made the holder of a present of game—and so on; any one with a little ingenuity can invent traps by the dozen, and the more peculiar they are, the greater the fun. The amusement may be still further increased by hiding the traps or presents all about the sitting-rooms of the house.

Now as to the presents themselves. It is always pleasant to be able to buy any we like, but nearly every one values more a gift that has been specially made for them than the smartest bought thing. So, little folk, let us set to work to think what we can make, how it is to be done, and for whom.

We ought to begin with grandpapa, who must have a warm pair of slippers of either knitted or wool work, and to show these off well he should be able to put his feet on a pretty round footstool, embroidered or braided for his use. One of the boys might carve him a paper-knife out of a piece of sandal-wood, with a fretwork handle; and a granddaughter could net or crochet him a long purse.

Grandmamma loves a warm quilted cape of some dark silk edged with fur, which one of the elder girls might make for her, whilst the little folk, with card tastefully painted, and bound with ribbon, can make a case for her spectacles or ball of wool when knitting ; or a large pincushion for her dressing-table, trimmed with lace, and with ribbons curled in bunches at the corners.

Papa likes a fretwork writing-case for his table, which the boys can make, mounting it neatly on leather, and putting in blotting-paper afterwards ; or a pair of warm knitted glove-mittens, manufactured by one of his little daughters.

For mamma there are many pretty things. The boys can give her ornamental brackets for her room, or frames for their own and sisters' photographs ; the elder sister should make her a lovely white satin sachet for her pocket-handkerchiefs, whilst the younger ones might accomplish a glove-box of painted card, wadded, and bound with ribbon.

Amongst the presents which deft-fingered older little folk can invent for each other are some of the following :—Glove, or handkerchief boxes (made of tinted or white card), paper and music cases, or work-baskets and spill-jars, all of which should be adorned by painting outside, and bound with bright-coloured ribbon. Spill-jars can be made by taking a piece of card about seven inches long by five and a half wide, and joining it very exactly, gumming one side a little bit over the other, so as to form a cylinder, and when dry, binding it neatly top and bottom with narrow ribbon. Cut out a perfectly round piece of card the size of the cylinder, and having bound that also, sew its edges with tiny stitches to the edges of the bottom of the jar, and it will be finished. You can make very pretty ones by painting them black, and putting sprays of dried leaves on them.

Nice writing-cases can be made of American cloth, stiffened with card, and lined with brown holland or silk, bound at the edges with strong ribbon ; the whole thing to be folded up, and secured with an elastic band. Pocket work-cases, for holding cotton, needles, thimble, and scissors, may be also made of American cloth, lined with silk.

Ornamental boxes filled with paper and envelopes, on which initial letters, monograms, or flowers have been painted, are always useful.

Boys often like to make a collection of stamps or monograms, and a book begun with some finished and half-finished designs for arranging them in is very acceptable, as is also a book made of flannel for keeping fishing-flies. Again, a little cabinet with drawers, nicely marked out in divisions, containing the beginning of a collection of coins,

minerals, sea-shells, or any other curiosities, gives much pleasure, and often leads a lad to take interest in the fairy realms of nature. Some little girls are fond of copying and keeping favourite pieces of poetry, therefore a book commenced with carefully drawn and painted borders of flowers, arabesques, or illuminations is a very welcome gift. Small botanical collections of sea-weed, flowers, ferns, or those most beautiful but little-thought-of plants—mosses, are a continual source of amusement.

Little girls who are clever with their needles may quickly make an exceedingly pretty apron, thus :— On a nice piece of black or dark silk or satin, lay across the lower half a variety of narrow coloured ribbons, some having a pattern on them. Work down their edges with silk braids, or feather-stitch in different and contrasting-coloured silks, also work in the middle of them fancy stitches, like stars, rounds, or crosses. When made up the effect is very bright and pretty. If there are pockets they should be trimmed in the same way.

Wicker-work baskets, when of a graceful shape, can be beautified by laying on a little way from the edge a two-inch crimped silk fringe in two colours, say pink or blue laid over white. The inside lining of blue or pink silk or satin must be either drawn up in a bag shape, or made into dainty pockets, with little ribbon bows on each. The handle must be decorated with the same fringes, which give the whole basket a soft, fluffy appearance.

Those who can make doll's clothes have many chances of giving acceptable presents, for a dollie with a complete wardrobe is most fascinating to any little girl, and a pleasant variety is made by dressing dolls in historical or foreign costumes.

Brush and shoe bags made in common crash, and embroidered in crewels with flowers or initials, are useful to every one, and even boys might manufacture them. As they all ought certainly to know how to net, and make artificial flies, they can always give a landing-net or a book of flies to their young fishermen friends, who highly prize such treasures.

Pincushions, mats, pen-wipers, and needle-books have not been mentioned, for they are generally almost troublesome by their numbers. It is, indeed, hardly necessary to enumerate more presents, for once ingenuity and invention are set working ideas come so fast that the Christmas cupboard or drawer is rapidly filled.

A. A. STRANGE BUTSON.

PLESSY'S CHRISTMAS EVE.

CHAPTER I.—THE LITTLE PATIENT.

PLESSY was ill, and it was Christmas Eve. Not so ill as to cause deep anxiety or require much attention. More was the pity! There would have been some consolation under those circumstances in not being very well. She was much too weak to get up from her little bed—too weak to trot along, as she loved to, in the clear white snow, or to join in any of the fun, which was all to take place away from home—too weak to do anything but feel the misfortune and the mistake it was to be unwell at such a season. Then her sickness made no difference to any one else : at least, although they all said they were sorry, and looked sorry, everything went on just the same as if she had been quite well.

There was Mrs. Cardigan's Christmas-tree party, to which she and her brothers and sisters were always invited, going to take place just as usual ; and there would be dancing and laughter and games and presents, exactly the same as there had been in the previous year, and for many years, when she was there to enjoy it all. Things didn't seem quite right to Plessy in some way. She could not understand it all, but she had a curious sort of feeling that because she was ill things ought not to go on in precisely the same manner as they did when she was well.

As she lay in her little bed under the nursery wall, she watched nurse wash and dress Mabel, and Charlie, and Harry, and little Rose, in their best evening frocks and knickerbocker suits, and listened to their joyous anticipations of the party with a curious little sense in her heart of the wrongness of everything. Nurse had constantly to subdue the happy exclamations of the rest with the reminder, "Poor Miss Plessy is ill, and can't bear any noise."

Then came papa's voice from the stairs, calling to nurse—"The carriage is at the door. Aren't the little ones ready ?"

"In a minute, sir," nurse responded.

And then on Plessy's thin white cheek four pairs of soft warm lips were eagerly pressed, one after the other, and "Good-night, Plessy ; don't be asleep when we come back," was whispered as the children hurried away.

Nurse cleared the nursery of the children's things, and set everything straight ; then she turned down the lamp, so that the white glow of the snow through the uncovered windows mingled with the soft yellow light.

Plessy remembered the year before, when she was one of the happy group below—the being muffled up in soft woollen and fur wraps by mamma and papa in the hall, and lifted into the close carriage—the banging-to of the door, the "All right !" given to Jessop, the coachman—and then the drive along the snow-covered road and up the long avenue of crystallised trees to the shining doorway of Mrs. Cardigan's big house, all the windows of which were ablaze with lights.

Presently, in amongst the nursery shadows Plessy's mamma glided. She was dressed in shimmering silk, with flowers in her hair. She and papa were going out to dine at the house of another friend. She too said, "Poor Plessy !" but in lower and more pitiful tones than nurse's.

"Don't be lonely, little one ; you will sleep and get strong for to-morrow, will you not ? You must be sure to be well enough for papa to carry you down to dinner, you know."

Then came papa himself, with his good-night kiss, and injunctions to go to sleep right away, and forget that it was Christmas Eve.

Plessy bravely kept back her tears until after her parents were gone, but she could not prevent the bright drops from falling then.

Nurse brought her supper soon after : a cup of beef tea and some thin strips of dry toast, which Plessy had to swallow in spite of the lump in her throat, which kept growing bigger instead of smaller.

When the cup was empty nurse straightened her pillows, tucked her up comfortably, put a fresh lump of coal on the fire, and turned the lamp very low. Then she bent over the little bed.

"Now you'll go to sleep, little lamb, won't you ?"

Plessy knew that nurse wanted to go down-stairs to supper, and that they would be merry down below, because it was Christmas Eve, and there was

no one in the house to be waited upon; so she answered meekly—

"I shan't want anything else to-night, nurse; you can go now."

"You'll be more likely to sleep if there's nobody in the room, Miss Plessy," said nurse, and left her.

So this was how Plessy spent her Christmas Eve.

CHAPTER II.—MRS. CARDIGAN'S PARTY.

How quiet the nursery was after nurse went, with the still gleam of mingled fire and lamp-light upon the old white pictured walls! The windows were covered now, and no snow-shine came in from without. And the snow, lying thickly outside in the streets, softened the rumble of the wheels of vehicles that passed.

Plessy's papa was a doctor, and lived almost in the centre of a large town, in a comparatively quiet street. The nursery was hardly ever free from noise, except when the little white beds ranged against the walls were all filled. Now they were empty, with smooth pillows that looked as though they were waiting for each little curly head. How loudly the clock ticked over the mantelpiece! Plessy had had no idea until then how very plainly it could make itself heard. It seemed almost to be speaking with the sharp click of its pendulum, if only she could have understood its language. Even the dropping of a cinder from the grate became a matter of importance now.

For a long while Plessy watched the shadows which the fire-light cast upon the walls, tracing fanciful figures in their dim shapes. But she grew tired of this occupation, and fell to thinking about Mrs. Cardigan's party of the year before, and wondering if this one would be half as nice. No other lady ever gave such nice parties as Mrs. Cardigan did in the estimation of little folks; no other Christmas-tree ever came up to hers, and to miss it was to miss the one pleasure of the winter for which no other could compensate.

In the previous year a young lady, a niece of Mrs. Cardigan's, had been visiting her, and she made an addition to the Christmas-tree which gave great delight, in the shape of a waxen fairy doll for its highest pinnacle. Plessy remembered how little Rose Cardigan had drawn her aside during an interval in the dances, and communicated this fact to her. From one to another the news of the fairy doll flew through the room.

Plessy recalled the thrill of anticipation which filled her own heart, and which was turned into a great longing when Rose further told her that the fairy doll was to be drawn for, and would become the absolute property of some little girl then present. Oh, if she might only be the fortunate little girl!

"Would there be a fairy of the tree this year?" Plessy asked of herself. And if so, would she be again drawn for? And who would win her? She would have no chance, and the year before it had been just as likely that the doll would fall to her as to any one else. She did not win her, but then she *might* have done.

The memory of the doll floated into her heart and mind now.

When supper was over, and the great folding-doors were flung open, revealing the large Christmas-tree, blazing with innumerable tapers and laden with glittering toys, Plessy's eyes had sought the topmost spray at once for the fairy. There it was, poised upon one waxen foot by a wire.

It was a lovely wax doll with streaming flaxen hair, upon which was set a crown of gold paper with five points. Its white gauze skirts were glittering with golden tinsel; and in its outstretched waxen arms it held a golden wand with a star and crescent at one end of it. The sweet face of the doll-fairy, with its deeply-fringed blue eyes, smiled down upon the upturned faces of all the little girls of the party, each of which had on it a longing to possess it.

Plessy kept her eyes fixed upon that topmost twig of the tree. None of the toy-fruit on the lower branches was to be compared for one moment with the doll.

When George Cardigan brought round the bag containing the tickets for the drawing, Plessy slipped in her little trembling hand with a great, almost irrepressible, wish swelling her heart. The tickets were made of cardboard, all cut exactly the same size, but on one of them was etched the figure of the doll, the rest all being blanks. The fortunate drawer of the etching became the possessor of the fairy from the tree.

In her nervous eagerness Plessy clutched one ticket and let it fall, then another, and drew it out. When George passed on with the silken bag to the little girl next to her, she stole a timid and furtive glance at the bit of cardboard in her hand.

The upper side was blank. With a thrill of fear she turned it over. The prize of the drawing had not fallen to her. She looked up once more to the tree. But she could not see the doll; her eyes were swimming with tears.

It had fallen to the share of little Agnes Moore, a child whose father was very rich, whose nursery was full of dolls, and who did not need this addition to them. It was a cruel thought to

"MABEL HAD A BOX . . . WHICH SHE PLACED ON PLESSY'S BED" (*p.* 332).

little Plessy that Agnes could never care for the doll as she would have done. Her papa was a hard-working doctor, and there were already five little children in his nursery, and such toys as they had to amuse them were principally of home manufacture. Her best doll had only a composition face, and nothing to speak of in the way of hair. Plessy had felt a sort of pitiful contempt for this homely doll ever since she had brought home with her from Mrs. Cardigan's party the memory of the fair hair and blue eyes of the waxen fairy of the tree. And her own doll had seemed, on its part, to have had a fit of the sulks. It had never wanted to be played with since, and seemed fully to understand that its little mistress's heart had changed towards it.

CHAPTER III.—PLESSY AND THE FAIRY.
SLOWLY the hours ticked on, and at last nurse came up. She thought Plessy was asleep, and stepped softly so as not to awaken her. From under her drooping eyelids Plessy watched her, thinking, as she saw her bright eyes, " She has had a pleasant Christmas Eve."

Nurse raked out the ashes from the grate, so that a little blaze sprang up and fresh shadows flickered on the walls. Then she turned down the coverlet of each little bed, and hung four little white-frilled night-dresses to the fire.

She had hardly finished these preparations when there was a sharp ring at the house door, quickly followed by the tramping of four pairs of dancing feet up the stairs, and voices talking about Plessy in no hushed tones.

Nurse rushed to the door, and Plessy heard her whispering to them to be quiet, " and not awaken poor Miss Plessy."

Plessy started upright in bed. " I am not asleep, nurse, and I want to hear all about the party."

In rushed four little happy figures, with tumbled hair and frocks, flushed faces and flashing eyes, and all talked at once, so that Plessy was quite bewildered.

Mabel had a box in her hands, which she placed on Plessy's bed, and all four were laden with toys, bon-bons, and trinkets. Mabel was by nature the most timid of the group, and it was some few minutes before she could make her little voice heard or attract Plessy's full attention.

"Tell me, tell me quickly!" cried Plessy, above the eager noise of the boys, who were displaying and explaining the novelty of their own Christmas-tree spoils. "Was there a fairy doll of the tree? and who won it in the raffle?"

"A fairy!" cried Charlie. "Of course there was; but who cares about that?"

"Please," exclaimed Mabel, pushing the long-shaped white box into a more conspicuous position before Plessy's eyes, "It's there; Mrs. Cardigan sent it to you, Plessy."

"I say, Pless, wasn't it jolly of her?" put in Charlie. "She wouldn't have the doll drawn for at all, but she said there was a little girl who was ill and couldn't come to the party, and it should be sent away to her."

"With Mrs. Cardigan's kind love," said Mabel; "and we are to tell you how very sorry she is that you have been lonely and ill on Christmas Eve."

"Oh!" cried Plessy, with a gasp of joy unspeakable, and her fingers fluttered with awe and trembling over the white lid, too feeble just at first, from the greatness of her surprise, to lift it.

"Come now, Master Harry; come now, Miss Mabel," cried nurse, "it's time you were all in bed. Why, it's close on ten o'clock, and Miss Plessy not asleep. How ever do you think she will be able to get up to-morrow?"

Mabel lingered to say to her sister, before following nurse to be undressed—

"Just look at her, Plessy! She's ever so much lovelier than the fairy doll was last year."

Plessy drew aside the lid, and there lay the object of her dreamful longings, all glittering in white and gold, with blue fringed eyes staring up placidly into her own. Slowly she lifted it out from its bed of soft wool; slowly she examined it. It was perfect in every remembered possession, from pink face to waxen toes, from flowing hair to white gauze robes and starry wand.

"Oh, how good of Mrs. Cardigan!" she exclaimed inwardly. "But I won't forget Who it was who put it into her heart to send the gift to me. Mamma says all kind thoughts come from Him."

She laid the little white doll down upon her pillow, closed her eyes and clasped her hands, while a fervent thanksgiving ascended to Him, the Lord of this happy Christmas-time.

Long after the four other little tired heads were slumbering on their respective pillows, Plessy's eyes sought to assure themselves of the possession of her treasure in the dim light of the silent nursery. She had not fallen asleep when the distant sound of voices broke upon the frosty stillness of the air with the familiar carol:—

"Good Christian men, rejoice, rejoice!"

The last sound she heard was the ringing of the bells that ushered in the Christmas morn; and, with their bright echoes in her heart, she wandered away into the land of dreams with her fairy doll of the Christmas-tree.

it! How kind every one was, what fun they had, and how quickly it was time to come home!

But it is by no means an easy thing to give a successful children's party. It is easy to fill the rooms with eager children, and to spread before them unusual and rich food, but the result of this is oftener than not weariness, fatigue, and dissatisfaction to the grown-up people, and discontent, disappointment, and even illness to the children. What can be more ridiculous than to collect together a crowd of children, of all ages and dispositions, to exchange for five or six hours their well-ventilated nurseries for heated rooms and draughty passages; their simple food for indigestible pastry and sickly, unwholesome sweets; their ordinary warm clothing for low-necked sleeveless dresses, which leave exposed that most sensitive part of the human frame, the upper part of the arms and the chest; and then to allow them to sit up for two or three hours beyond their usual time for retiring, until the fashionable hour arrives for children's parties to break up, when, worn out with fatigue and excitement, the little ones are carried off to bed?

This is not the sort of thing I mean by a well-conducted children's party, and fortunately a great many sensible parents see the evils of which I have spoken, and set their faces against them. At the same time it is by no means necessary, for those who wish to give pleasure to their children without harming them either morally or physically, to debar them altogether from attending gatherings of the kind; and common-sense people, of whom there are a great many in the world, would confer a benefit on their friends and acquaintance if they would show them by their example how these pleasant little reunions can be managed in a common-sense way.

For one thing, it is very important not to invite a larger number of children than the size of the rooms will comfortably accommodate. This mistake is frequently made, and it is a very unfortunate one. It oftener than not arises from the desire of the hostess to pay off her visiting debts all at once, and so she asks

HOW TO GIVE A CHILDREN'S PARTY.

"THE children are going to a party." I hope there are not many mothers and not many children, in the homes which this Magazine enters, who do not understand the meaning of this phrase. The young ones look forward to the treat for days before, with that ecstatic anticipation of coming joy which is felt only by the young. When the day dawns the hours seem as if they would never drag their weary length along, for it is felt to be worse than useless to attempt any ordinary employment or amusement. And when the party is over, what delight there is in talking about every child whose parents she wishes to compliment, and the consequence is that there is no enjoyment; the rooms are unpleasantly crowded, and filled with children who have no sympathy with one another, who have not even room to make acquaintance, and so become cross and bad-tempered, and ten to one ill-behaved.

It is a great mistake, too, to ask a number of very young children to parties. After sunset the little ones are best in bed. Every one knows they are invited with the object of pleasing their mothers, but sensible mothers would take a greater pleasure in seeing them warmly tucked up in their soft little cots, than in having them ever so much admired at unseasonable times.

The hours for meeting and parting must necessarily vary with the habits of the children; for even children's habits vary, and no hard and fast line could possibly be drawn. Nevertheless the custom, which is unfortunately too common, of keeping up children's parties until a late hour cannot be sufficiently deprecated. The only effect of it is that the children are upset in health and temper. They do not enjoy themselves any more than they would do if they met early and retired early; and they are unfitted the next day for both work and play. This practice has done more than anything else to make prudent parents object to children's parties.

It is of no use to expect that when the children have arrived they will amuse themselves. They will not. If left to do so, the boys will gradually collect in one part of the room, and, I am afraid, will sometimes conduct themselves rather roughly; and the girls will sit modestly and silently in another part, scarcely speaking a word. It needs a grown-up person possessed of both energy and kindliness, and who has made up his or her mind that hard work will be required, both to begin the enjoyment and to keep it up. It is the best thing to draw up a programme beforehand, and to have all the details arranged; and it requires forethought and care to see that there is no hitch in them. Of course the most delightful plan is to have a special entertainment provided for the children—a conjurer to puzzle them, or a show of some kind for them to watch. It is not every one, however, who can afford to pay a professional person to undertake the management of it; and it must be properly carried out, or it is worse than nothing. What can be more wearisome than to sit in a darkened room watching an inexperienced amateur try to exhibit a magic lantern? An oily smell, suggestive of headache, fills the apartment; the spectators are anxiously waiting for the sight, when a black figure is seen to rush through the darkness, to seek somewhere for something which has been forgotten, and which is not found, and for want of which the pictures look like nothing but an illuminated haze, indistinct and unsatisfactory. The politer members of the company do their best to admire, but at the same time feel immensely relieved when the impracticable machine is removed, and an ordinary round game is called for.

Of late years Christmas-trees have become very popular at children's parties. They are exceedingly pretty, and when tastefully trimmed with glittering ornaments, and lighted up with small lamps or candles, have a very charming appearance. When more than this is attempted, however, I think they are a mistake. Ticketed presents for the children are often hung upon the tree, and corresponding tickets drawn for. I have scarcely ever known this plan successful. In nine cases out of ten the boys get the dolls, and the girls the cricket-balls; and one difference between children and grown-up people is that the former find more difficulty in hiding their feelings than the latter. The kind host and hostess give themselves a great deal of trouble, and put themselves to expense, and after all only succeed in making their guests discontented and dissatisfied.

If it is wished to make presents to the children, why not have a bran-pie?—that is, a large box filled with bran, in which is hidden a present specially designed for each child, and marked with his name, and which is sought for by the youngest guest present. Or let one of the grown-up people dress like an old man, and come in laden with the treasures. All sorts of similar plans might be adopted, but it is not well to leave the distribution of the presents to chance.

One of the most successful parties that my children ever attended was given by a clever and rather eccentric friend of mine. In issuing her invitations, she requested that the children might arrive not later than three, and be sent for not later than eight o'clock. When they arrived, they were shown into a large, comfortable room, and the hostess and a lady friend joined with them in playing at old-fashioned round games, which were continued after tea. About half-past seven the children were taken into another room, and invited to seat themselves round a large table. In the middle of this was a Christmas-tree, prettily lighted and tastefully decorated. A plate was set for each child, upon which was an orange, a piece of cake, and a few raisins, and by the side of the plate a small parcel containing a present. Upon the parcel was placed a doll's candlestick, holding a small wax taper, lighted. The children examined their presents and partook of their refreshment by the light only of the candles and the Christmas-tree, and their delight was unbounded.

There is one word that must be said to parents in speaking of children's parties. When children receive an invitation to a party, the object of those who give it can only be either to give pleasure to the children, or to compliment the parents. In return for this they have a right to expect that they shall be treated fairly. This cannot be said to be the case if the children when they leave home are not perfectly well. So many of the complaints peculiar to children are spread by carelessness of this kind; and what can be more annoying to a host and hostess than to find that their house has been the centre from which illness has spread to their friends?

PHILLIS BROWNE.

THE FIRST SNOWFALL.

THE leafless trees were black and wet,
   Half hid in chilly mist, last night—
This morn each wears a coronet,
   With purest crystal fires alight.

We in the dark with dreams were still,
   When silently the elves came down,
To throw a great robe round the hill,
   And muffle all the sleeping town.

The sceptre is in Winter's hand—
   His willing troop of Northern fays
Have thrown his jewels o'er the land,
   In their enchanted midnight maze.

The hall seems, as it stands alone
   With red sun on its frosted panes,
Like a palace to dreamers shown
   In a proud fairy lord's domains.

Here is the robin, welcome guest;
   And he is cheerful in the flaw—
The amulet upon his breast
   Will shield him in the icy shaw.

Bright bird, you bring again the joys
   That made us happy long ago,
When we were little girls and boys—
   When first we saw you in the snow.

How merry will the children be
   When they awake! It makes me smile
To think how they will shout to see
   All things white for many a mile!

What a sweet wonder is the year,
   With seasons charming all our days!
We wait for Winter with some fear,
   But beauty is in all his ways.

GUY ROSLYN.

CATERING FOR CHILDREN'S PARTIES.

BY A. G. PAYNE, M.A., AUTHOR OF "COMMON-SENSE COOKERY," ETC.

IT is a common saying, "There are no children now-a-days," and in arranging for children's evening parties, so common at the present season of the year, we—and by we I mean what children call grown-up people—must be careful not to fall into the mistake that Miss Pinkerton made when she presented the youthful Becky Sharp with a doll. I recollect not long ago seeing a picture of a little boy who has come home late, leaning back in an easy chair. His elder sister suggests that he should have a piece of cake and go to bed. The boy, who is apparently about ten, however replies, "I should like a lobster salad and some beer."

I must not, however, forget my subject ; though, of course, we cannot have children's parties if there are no children. The fact is, there are plenty of children, only children are very different now from what they used to be years ago. Fortunately, I am going to confine myself to the eating and drinking part of the entertainment, and will leave the children and their elders to manage the games as best they can, merely remarking as one of the signs of the times, that it will often be seen that persons, say between forty and fifty, who are present in order to help to amuse, really enjoy themselves and the games too, while young men and women of thirteen get rather bored than otherwise with the proceedings generally.

In one respect I think it will be found that the children of the present age resemble the children of all ages, viz., in considering the supper the event of the evening ; and I think I can safely pass over the tea and coffee part of the business by saying that more will take coffee than tea, that it is incredible what a lot of thin bread-and-butter children will eat, and that if there is plenty of it, many will refuse the cake altogether. This latter is different from what it used to be years ago.

Next, the supper. And let us always bear one point in mind—we must do our best to please both the palate and the eye, but at the same time endeavour that no one child present shall feel any the worse for the meal the next morning.

First remember, unless the children are very young indeed, that many are accustomed to have a late dinner, far more often than was customary years ago, and that on the present occasion they have dined early. This, coupled with the fact that time should always be allowed for digestion, tends to show us how desirable it is not to have supper too late. It is far better for children to have an hour or two of play after supper, than for them to go home almost immediately and go to bed. Boys at school go out into the cricket field directly after a heavy dinner of hot meat and pudding, and are never the worse for the exercise. So, too, it will be found that children enjoy the games

even more after supper than before it. In fact, after supper it will be seen that children will be more like children.

Now, it will never do to let children make a heavy meal off sweets and pastry, so let each one begin with some cold fowl or cold turkey, or at any rate with some meat sandwiches. First, the cold fowl and turkey. These should be roasted the day before, and should be glazed and ornamented. A very good and simple glaze can be made as follows :—Slice an onion, and put it into half a pint of water with a little parsley, let it boil for some time and strain it off, then add a good tea-spoonful, or rather more, of Liebig's extract of meat, a little pepper and salt, and dissolve in it about $\frac{3}{4}$ oz. of gelatine ; one yolk of an egg may be added. The extract of meat is quite enough to make it of a nice rich brown colour, though some persons add colouring, which is generally burnt sugar and water, and what professionals call "Black Jack." This, when cold, will of course be a firm jelly. All that is necessary is to paint the cold fowls, turkey, &c., with this when it is nearly cold, but not set. This glaze will set almost directly it is put on. Avoid, however, glazing the fowls or turkey on the dish on which they will be served up. Have plenty of bright fresh green double parsley, and if possible a few cut flowers. One of the best accompaniments to cold fowl, is cold tongue. If the tongue be a fresh one it should be glazed like the fowl ; but what will be found now to be very good, and far cheaper, are the preserved tongues in tins. Cut the tin neatly round close to the edge, and turn it out on a dish. Cut off the top slice with a very sharp knife, and surround the rolled tongue with a frilled paper, which had better be tied on with some white cotton. These tinned tongues are decidedly lighter than fresh ones. A border of thick green parsley outside the frill will improve the appearance of the dish.

Sandwiches, properly made, will always be found popular at evening parties. Beef sandwiches are so easily made that they scarcely need directions, but I would remind you that a square tinned loaf is best ; very little butter indeed should be used, and if the weather is cold the butter must be put in a warm place for some time, or else the bread will crumple in spreading the butter. Boiled silver-side of beef (fresh) is best, and a very little mustard and pepper should be added. A novelty in the way of sandwiches can be made with tinned preserved salmon, and by using mayonnaise sauce instead of butter. First make some good thick mayonnaise sauce, by dropping oil drop by drop on the yolk of an egg, carefully separated from the white, and beating it with a fork. Do not use any vinegar or pepper and salt at starting, or you will probably fail. Keep adding the oil and beating till the mixture gets as thick as butter. Now add some tarragon vinegar, about a tea-spoonful will be enough, and a little white pepper and salt. Butter some thin slices of bread with this sauce and place a very thin layer of salmon between them, having first thoroughly pounded the salmon in a mortar or basin, and then, after gently pressing the slices of bread together, cut the slices into little triangular pieces, and pile them up on a plate and ornament the dish with nice bright parsley, and place a few small crayfish, with outstretched claws, round the base, and one on the top. It is a pretty, delicious, and inexpensive dish. Prawns, good-sized ones, are even better than crayfish.

Lobster salads are very nice and very popular, but I should advise not having any at children's parties. Before we come to the sweets we will for one moment consider the somewhat difficult question of what is best to drink. Plain water is decidedly best. Cham-

and purchase ¼ lb. of angelica ; pick a thick piece, the darker the green the better—this will cost 6d. ; ¼ lb. of preserved cherries, another 6d. ; and a small bottle of cochineal. It is wonderful what an improvement can be made in the appearance of dishes with these simple ornaments.

Let us take the simple case of a boiled custard pudding that has been turned out of a shape. To illustrate the point, I will take a very common shape, that will probably be found in every house—viz., an empty round marmalade pot. First, the pudding : suppose you are going to make several, you need not use too many eggs, but can, if you wish it, make the puddings less rich by using a little corn-flour as well. Essence of vanilla is a most delicious flavouring, but I think it will be found that children as a rule do not care for vanilla, and I would strongly recommend the

A MERRY PARTY.

pagne is expensive and unnecessary. Port wine negus is very nice, but not exactly suitable with meat. Many children will drink water, or a little sherry and water ; but for moderately-sized children, who do not care to take water, what can be better than plain home-made lemonade ? To my thinking a glass of lemonade is far preferable to *cheap* champagne, and far less vulgar. Why poison your guests for the sake of appearances? Claret cup is a nice thing, but more suitable for summer than winter. A good claret cup can be made as follows :—A bottle of sound claret, free from all acidity, about eight lumps of sugar, which can be dissolved in a little boiling water first, the rind of half a lemon, one glass of golden sherry, a strip of cucumber-peel put in for five minutes and then taken out again, a small glass of Maraschino, a lump of ice, and two bottles of soda-water. Balm and borage are generally recommended to be added, but are by no means necessary.

We now come to the sweets, and I would remind you that a really nice supper very much depends upon appearances. A day or two before the supper, go out

good old-fashioned flavouring of bay-leaves, two or three of which should be washed, and then boiled in the milk used for the pudding for a short time. We will, however, suppose the pudding made, and turned out into a glass dish. Now take the angelica, and cut it first into very thin slices, and out of these slices cut some strips just like blades of grass, pointed at the end. On the top of the round mould of pudding place a single preserved cherry, and make it the centre of a small star composed of strips of angelica, and see what a different aspect the mould has. In fact, it has the appearance known as "coming from the pastrycook's." A row of preserved cherries can be placed round the edge of the mould, though it is a doubtful improvement. A nice, clear, bright, pink sauce can be poured round the edge, made as follows :— Boil a little water, add some lump sugar to it, and a piece of lemon-peel ; thicken it with a little arrowroot till it looks like syrup, colour it with a few drops of cochineal, and add about a table-spoonful of Scotch whiskey ; let it get cold, and pour it round the solid custard pudding.

A very nice mould can be made out of an old York-shire-pie dish. These are generally quite plain ovals, about six inches long and four inches wide. In placing a star in the centre of this, the strips of angelica pointing long-ways should be, of course, longer than those pointing cross-ways; or, in other words, the star should be arranged in proportion to the shape of the pudding.

It will be found a great convenience using these shapes for making plain puddings, as the ordinary shapes will very likely be wanted for jellies, lemon sponges, &c.

One very popular dish at supper-parties is tipsy-cake. I think tipsy-cake is best made from small penny sponge-cakes. These can be first sliced and spread with thin layers of raspberry jam, and moistened with some sweet wine, such as raisin, suitable for children. Avoid, in any case, a dry sherry. Next have ready some custard, and in making this I would strongly advise Swiss milk instead of sugar. Take, say, a pint of milk and boil it; stir in a good table-spoonful of Swiss milk, and when it is thoroughly dissolved add four eggs well beaten up; put it all together in a jug, and place the jug in boiling water, and keep stirring till the custard is sufficiently thick, but do not go on too long, or it will curdle. Custard for tipsy-cake should be thick, or it will, when poured over the sponge-cakes, run off and leave them bare. When the custard is thick enough (if you wish it very thick, a little corn-flour mixed smooth with some cold water may be cautiously added), take the jug out of the boiling water and plunge it into cold water, and keep stirring for some time, as otherwise the custard has a tendency to turn lumpy. When the custard is quite cold it can be poured over the sponge-cakes, which have been piled up on a glass dish; but put off pouring the custard as long as possible.

The dish has now to be ornamented, and the usual ornaments are almonds sliced, stuck into the cakes, and which are allowed to stick out porcupine fashion. These almonds must first be thrown into hot water, the skins rubbed off, and then thrown into cold water in order to preserve their white colour. This decoration can of course be varied. Some of the thin strips of almond can be coloured pink with cochineal, and can be mixed with the white strips of almond, as well as some thin strips of angelica; but pink and green must be used sparingly always in ornamenting dishes.

Some tiny pieces of angelica can be sprinkled over the custard instead of any almonds being used at all, similar to chopped parsley over a mayonnaise salad.

One very popular supper dish with children is trifle. It is rather expensive if made properly, but sponge-cakes can be mixed with the macaroons and ratafias, and whipped white of egg can be used instead of whipped cream for the top. White of egg is not so nice, but it is far cheaper and less rich than cream.

Whipped white of egg will be found an excellent thing to use for garnishing dishes, and if it is made nice and stiff, so that those little sugar-plums called "hundreds and thousands" can be sprinkled over it,

the effect will be very pretty. For instance, a little drop of white froth can be placed in the centre of each pippin in a dish of stewed Normandy pippins, and then a little pinch of sugar-plums placed on the top. Do not, however, sprinkle the hundreds and thousands till as late as possible.

A great many nice dishes can be made in the pre-sent day with the assistance of fruits preserved in tins, and I would particularly mention preserved peaches and apricots. For instance, take a tin of the former and strain off the peaches; add a little wine to the syrup, and dissolve in it, by boiling gently, enough gelatine to make it a fairly firm jelly when cold. The quantity of gelatine is generally about 2 oz., or rather more, to a quart of liquid. A few drops of cochineal may be added to make it red, and the liquid must be then poured into a mould, and the peaches dropped in. When quite cold, you have a nice mould of peach jelly with ripe peaches in it. It must, however, be made slightly stiffer than ordinary jelly, as the slices of peaches inside increase the tendency it has to break. This jelly of course will not be bright, though it can be made nearly clear by means of white of egg used in the ordinary manner.

Of course you must have some pastry for children's suppers, but let it consist as much as possible of fruit pies rather than jam tarts, puffs, &c.

One very nice supper-sweet is rice-cakes made as follows:—Get some plain rice, wash it, and boil till it is quite tender; drain, and mix it with some eggs well beaten up in milk, in the same proportion as used for making ordinary custard. This can be flavoured with vanilla, bay-leaves, essence of almonds, or with lemon-peel—this latter flavour being best obtained by rubbing lumps of sugar on the rind of a lemon and afterwards dissolving the sugar in the milk. Put the rice, mixed with the custard, into a tin to bake, first of all taking the usual precaution to butter the tin. A large square tin is best, so that the rice-cake, when baked, will be about an inch thick. The process of baking will harden the cake, which can be turned out whole when cold, but not before, and can then be cut into any shape desired. You can make round cakes with a cutter (but this is wasteful), or square cakes by simply cutting with a knife. Perhaps the best way is to cut them into strips, which can be piled up like children build a tower with toy bricks. The cakes and strips are best ornamented with jam and marma-lade, laying on streaks of alternate colours. These cakes look very pretty, and have the advantage of being very light and wholesome.

Try and avoid letting children, especially young ones, finish up with rather sour oranges and hard apples, intermixed with the sugar-plums out of the crackers. Too often it will be found that these things do what mischief there is done on these occasions. If you have them on the table to make a show, recol-lect it is hard to refuse them to any little one. In conclusion, think of the children's health and comfort rather than of making the table "look handsome" to gratify your own vanity.

HOW THE CHRISTMAS CARDS ARE MADE.

A · BROTHER'S · CHRISTMAS · GREETING.

A PLEASANT sound of many voices, that rises and falls as a door is opened and shut, like the effect produced by raising the louvres, or shutters, in the swell of an organ; then a merry laugh or outcry, and then, as we enter, a complete silence, save for the scratching of busy fingers over paper. To a certain extent it is like entering a school-room with Madame the principal; but this is no school, only a light, well-ventilated work-room, in which some fifty or sixty girls are as busy as the bees in some hive—the bees whose hum seemed to issue from this hive of industry.

Those who take an interest in seeing girls and women furnished with the means of gaining a respectable livelihood in some clean, light business, would be delighted here. For there is not a sallow, unwholesome face to be seen; no girl seems drooping over too much work in a close room, but all look bright, cheerful, and happy, their eyes directing their busy fingers, while a staid middle-aged female sits at a kind of desk in a stall, as if

playing at selling the brightly coloured pictures about her to the various girls who come and go. But this seeming play is all in earnest, and every movement here is relative to the great commercial power, business; for though it is a bright, sunshiny, autumn day, these are preparations for Christmas; in fact, this is one of those factories of Christmas Cards, visited to obtain the materials for a description of the little artistic works with which our homes are flooded at the festive time.

It is of very modern growth, this sending of Christmas tokens; and in spite of the very severe letters that have appeared in the daily press, it is a plant of healthy and ever-increasing dimensions. In fact, it seems that this year there will be a great advance in quantity and quality, for the various makers have been enlisting the services of artists of no mean position, with the result that some of the cards, small as they are, display pictures of such refinement and delicacy of treatment that they will be well worthy of preservation. Let us see how these cards are prepared.

Accompanying a guide to a lower room, where men and boys only are employed, we see a number of great, heavy, creamy-coloured stones, like the flags used for paving, but much thicker, and with one side exquisitely smooth. These are German lithographic stones, and on a closer inspection we find them covered with designs. In fact, an artist has painted on paper some charming little scrap, perhaps a bullfinch on a spray of holly, and this has been copied by the lithographic artists, and, to use their term, placed upon the stone. Let us watch the work, and see what that means.

Here is what has been done. Ten stones will be required to print this pretty design, and on examining them we see that something resembling a badly defined or shadowed resemblance of the pretty card is on these stones; not once, but sixty-four times repeated—eight rows and eight columns of birds placed

MAY · CHRISTMAS · PLEASURES · AWAIT · YOU.

here by printing or transferring on the stones. It seems a great number, and a great amount of preparation, but we soon learn that it is needful, and that the repetitions of what seem trifles result in the per-

LET · TREASVRES · FILL · Ye · CHRISTMAS · STOCKING.

fection we see. The object is, of course, to produce the one brightly-coloured drawing of the water-colour artist in endless quantities, and so at the different presses this is done.

At one the smooth, pure white sheets of card are brought in contact with the stone, and they come up with a bordering of gold. At another press an outline blue pattern is printed on the ground of gold. At the next, a dark shading to the blue pattern, and in the middle of each card a dull dark patch, and a faint trace of a spray. Next follow the shape of the bird, the dark head and back, the delicate roseate hue of its breast, the bright green and dark green of the holly, the scarlet of the berries, and so on and on, each stone supplying some one touch of colour, till lying before us is, in all its original beauty, the reproduction of the artist's water-colour painting, repeated here sixty-four times, and being produced by this combination of labour, after the long preparation, in thousands upon thousands.

Here, though, lies a heap of sheets of cards of a very charming but simple design. It is merely a full-blown rose. Its shadows are delicate in tint, and the whole is very beautiful ; but its beauties are yet to be heightened by bringing them out in low relief. In fact, these cards are to be embossed, and to do this a steel die has been cut of the shape of the rose with all its petals. This die is attached to a die-press of tremendous power, a couple of heavy balls fly round,

the screw-press descends on the printed roses, and when the card is removed, the petals and buds stand out above the paper with admirable effect.

This embossing is carried to a great pitch of perfection—faces, figures, and various designs being treated in this way ; but a vast amount of the work is done abroad, cut out by steel dies, and sent over here to supply manufacturers at a far lower cost than they can get the labour done at here. It is this same principle of stamping with steel dies, each of which is laboriously cut in some intricate design, at great expense, that supplies us with the delicate paper-lace work that so charmingly ornaments many of the so-called cards, while much of the work is cut out on the same principle—that is, the driving down of a steel die by means of a fly-wheel, or a couple of heavy flying balls, which are attached to the die-armed screw, and twist it down.

The printing in colours of all the cards is executed on the same principle. The more colours in a card, the more tints even and shades of the same colour, the more stones it has taken, and consequently the more printings it has received. But these sheets of twenty-fours or forty-eights or sixty-fours, according to the size of the designs, are broad and large. They have been rolled and pressed, and look the very perfection of beauty as they are passed over to a man ready to do execution upon them, for he presides over a guillotine. This is a machine set to the exact gauge of the length of the cards to be, and taking forty or fifty, or maybe a hundred sheets, the workman lays them flat on the machine table, passes them under till they are stopped by the gauge, runs round a couple of balls

LET · VS · SHARE · Ye · FRUIT · OF · Ye · XMAS · TREE.

which turn a screw to hold them tight, and then a wheel revolves, the guillotine knife comes down with a steady, lateral descent, and cuts through the hard mass of pressed-together cards as easily as if they were so much cheese. By this process the card of sixty-four designs is cut up into equal rows of eight, and these in turn are cut into the single cards so familiar at Christmas time, and with edges so regular and smooth that no knife or scissors will produce the same effect. A man so employed cuts up countless thousands in a day, a few turns of a wheel regulating his machine to suit cards of any size ; and these now cut up are passed to an upper room, where busy-fingered girls packet them in assorted dozens — fastening each packet with a pretty ornamental band of paper, whose ends are rapidly secured with a touch of molten sealing-wax.

Passing up-stairs once more, we are led into the room where so many girls are busy, some making the packets, but the greater portion at much more elaborate work ; and we learn that they far excel boys in these tasks, from their deft cleverness of finger, cleanliness, and closer application to the duty in hand. One girl here has before her a number of cards with so many pretty borders, but blank in the centre. Over this blank place she fits a pretty design in lace-paper, which is made to stand away from the base by four paper springs, formed by doubled strips of the width of narrow tape. Another has a box full of stamped flowers, which she rapidly gums on her cards. Another has birds, the robin being the favourite, and it is wonderful to see how the red-breasted bird, stamped out and embossed, is placed in position with a rapid touch of a gum-brush, and laid in a heap with others to dry. And so card after card is built up with embossed ornaments according to its price, some being quite elaborate pieces of workmanship, all lace, gilding, silvering, and brilliant colours, like one of the better-class valentines meant for a later season.

As a matter of course, the emblems of Christmas time form the majority of the designs for cards ; holly is abundant, with its dark glistening leaves and scarlet berries ; and so is mistletoe, all delicate grey-green and luminous pearl. The Christmas rose too is plentiful, and every floral design is in exquisite taste, and marvellous in its fidelity to nature. But wassail-bowls and ruddy Father Christmases are not wanting, with fir-trees out of number. Wondrous plum-puddings, each with a knife and fork in it, lie heaped in a box, ready for gumming on some of the cards ; in another box are comical turkeys and stately pigs, but the serious and pretty have the greatest sway, while nothing is seen that would offend the most fastidious taste.

Here are some quaint cards, evidently intended for a novelty for the children. They consist of figures which are at first represented by faces, hands, and legs, but which a nimble-fingered damsel dresses up with little stamped velvet suits of clothes, taking them rapidly from a box, and gumming them in their places with a delicacy of touch and accuracy of eye that are in truth surprising. Next to her a quiet-looking girl is

fitting together card-fans, each leaf of the fan bearing a calendar printed ready for the New Year, 1879. They are pretty designs, these, and combine the useful with the ornamental, though from their fragile structure the latter must prevail.

There is a pleasant odour here, though, as if the mimic flowers that flash in myriad dyes had assumed the real at the touch of some enchanter's wand. Rose, lily, musk, and verbena, what a sweet blending ! It is only, however, the girl who makes up the sachets or scent-packets distributing perfume, Flora-like, as she hastens on her work. Her scent-packets are, so to speak, so many glazed or enamelled envelopes, with a Christmas card where the direction should be. Into each of these, the Christmas card Flora places a little cotton-wool or wadding, just dusted over with the scent-powder, fastens securely the lappet, and there is a pretty Christmas present, odorous and sweet, ready to remind its recipient of the giver with a strange and subtle power of its own. It is for this reason probably that the forget-me-not, with its tiny eyes of blue, is so often a portion of the design outside, even though a kindly wish for the coming season leaves the gentle flower in the shade.

One firm has excelled itself in the beauty of some of its productions. No built-up pictures are here, all embossing and separate designs, but charming artistic designs, many being gems of the most exquisite tinting and effect. For instance, they have prepared a series of studies of girl-life, simple and classic as if from the pencil of Alma Tadema. Another series is of Japanese birds, leaves, and flowers, delicately quaint, and though perhaps bordering on the grotesque, yet so beautiful in conception that the eye does not weary, as it is never offended by a garish hue.

Perhaps the most perfect of these real gems of colour-printing are the birds, which are so true to nature, so harmonious in tint, that none but an artist who is a naturalist as well could have produced the effect. The aim seems to have been more to obtain a pleasing picture than to produce anything related to the festive season. Hence we have sea-anemones, orchids, and cacti horrent with spines, and quaint in shape; flowers of tints such as nature might have dyed ; and mingled with these a series of wild dreams of fairy and elf land, with wondrously formed birds and quadrupeds, such as must have come from the brain of Ernest Griset, though they are unsigned.

Seen in their perfection of blended colours, the cards are very beautiful ; in their earlier stages of production, however, they are so many puzzles, and a half-blank sheet with a few colours apparently daubed here and there is anything but a pleasing object to the eye. It is not until lithographic stone after stone has added its blending touches that we realise the patience, care, and wonderful exactitude that have to be exercised to produce these trifles of the season, many of which are really high-class works of art.

But the hum of voices has suddenly increased as we are deeply studying one of a heap of pictures being formed into packets, the scene being a sailors' mess, with the Jack at the head cutting the Christmas pudding, and this brings us back to the fact that it is one o'clock, and dinner-time, the girls hurrying away to their midday meal, evidently light-hearted and happy at the coming of this respite from their daily task, one that gives pleasure to old and young throughout the land.

The silhouette studies we have given with this paper are original designs supplied by our own artist for the delectation of the readers of this Magazine. Some of our younger readers may find a pleasurable employment in taking tracings or pen-and-ink copies of them, and sending them to their friends.

CHRISTMAS GAMES FOR EVERYBODY.

BRILLAT-SAVARIN, the great gastronomist, said that "to invite a person to your house is to take charge of his happiness while under your roof." We will invite our friends this Christmas-time —we will take charge of their happiness for awhile, and as we feel that the responsibility is a grave one, and that we should be very sorry if they failed to enjoy themselves whilst under our care, we will lay our plans for their gratification beforehand. We will store our memories with a catalogue of games, and Christmas diversions, and surely we shall be able to think of something that will suit the fancy of one and all.

There are some games that seem to belong peculiarly to Christmas, and foremost amongst these is the game of " Snapdragon."

> " Here he comes with flaming bowl,
> Don't he mean to take his toll,
> Snip ! Snap ! Dragon !
> Take care you don't take too much,
> Be not greedy in your clutch,
> Snip ! Snap ! Dragon !
>
> " With his blue and lapping tongue
> Many of you will be stung,
> Snip ! Snap ! Dragon !
> For he snaps at all that comes,
> Snatching at his feast of plums,
> Snip ! Snap ! Dragon !"

When this pastime is decided upon, a number of raisins are put into a large, broad, shallow bowl, and a little brandy or other spirit is poured over the fruit. The lights in the room are then extinguished, the spirit is ignited, and the bystanders in turns plunge their hands through the flames and endeavour to obtain possession of the fruit. This, of course, is not easily done ; it requires both nerve and agility, and the unavailing attempts of the company cause a good deal of fun. Added to this, the burning spirit gives a lurid glare which lights up the eager faces of the guests, and has quite a weird-like effect.

This game has been played at Christmas from time immemorial. It is declared to have been invented by Hercules, who, when "he had slain the flaming dragon of Hesperia, made a fiery dish of the apples grown in the orchard, which dish he named Snapdragon." In the western counties of England it is played under a varied form and known under a slightly different name, that of *Flapdragon*. In this game a lighted candle is put into a can of ale or cider, and attempts are made to drink the liquor while the candle is still burning. This is not done without the face being either blackened or slightly burnt.

Some games, which are rather boisterous in their character, are known to every one and need no description. Amongst these are " Blind Man's Buff," " Puss in the Corner," " Trencher," " Blind Postman," " Hunt the Slipper ;" and " The Elements," or " Air, Earth, Fire, and Water." " Proverbs," too, is a capital old game. When it is played, one member

39

of the company leaves the room, and the rest fix upon a well-known proverb. The banished guest returns, and asks each person a question, who in reply is bound to bring in one word of the proverb in its proper order, and the questioner tries to find out from these answers what the proverb is. A very amusing variety of this game is called "Shooting Proverbs." The guests each appropriate one word of the proverb as before. The one who is trying to guess the proverb comes in, steps into the middle of the room, and calls out in a commanding voice, "Make ready! Present! Fire!" At the word "Fire" all the company shout their own words at once, and the proverb is to be guessed from the sound, which is a very confusing one.

Perhaps there is no game which gives greater amusement both to young folks and old ones than the game of "Characters," sometimes called "Twenty Questions," and sometimes "Nouns." In this, one of the company thinks of some one particular person or thing, and the others ply him with questions, and endeavour to find out his secret from the answers. It is astonishing how judicious questioning can draw the most out-of-the-way object out of mystery into the light of day. Sometimes the company divide themselves into two parties, each of which sends out one of their number, and on his return questions him separately, and endeavours to find out his secret before the other side can do so. Each candidate must be questioned by the opposite side, and the party which first guesses rightly takes possession of both candidates. That side is considered to have won the game which draws over the largest number of members. When played in this way, this game is often called "Clumps."

"Trades" is a very amusing game. In this, each person chooses a certain trade, and one member of the company who is named by the rest makes up a story, in the course of which he introduces an account of his shopping excursions, and calls haphazard upon the representative of each business to name some noun which belongs to his trade. Thus: a butcher is to name a certain joint of meat, a grocer some article of grocery, and so on. No item is to be mentioned twice, and if there is any attempt to do so, or if there is any hesitation in naming something suitable, a forfeit must be paid. When the story is well told, a good deal of fun may be got out of this game.

"Dumb Crambo" is another good game. When playing it half the party leave the room, and those who remain choose a verb, which the others are to guess. When the absent ones return they are told of a word which will rhyme with the word fixed upon, and they then consult together to find out what it is. Instead of *speaking* their guess they *act* it. If they guess rightly they are applauded; if they fail they are hissed. A word spoken on either side, excepting by the actors for the purpose of private consultation, entails a forfeit.

A very old, but a very amusing game, is "Simon." Simon is chosen from the company. He and the rest of the players seat themselves in a circle round the fire, and Simon gives his commands. If he prefaces them by the words "Simon says," they are to be obeyed however ridiculous they may be. If these important words are omitted, the commands are not to be obeyed and any one who acts upon them must withdraw from the contest. When Simon is clever and quick of speech this game makes great fun, and it is very absurd to see a large company imitating his movements. "Simon says, Thumbs up. Simon says, Thumbs down. Simon says, Touch your hair. Simon says, Touch your boots. Simon says, Stop touching your boots; touch your boots again——" Some one is sure to be caught.

"Shadow Buff" is a pretty variety of "Blind Man's Buff," and it is a safe, quiet, and pretty game for young people. If there is a white curtain in the room, it should be fastened down to make a smooth surface. If there is no curtain, a sheet or a table-cloth will be required. The one who is to be blind man seats himself before the curtain with his back to his companions, and to the light. The rest pass behind him so that their shadows may be thrown upon the white surface, and the one whom he names from the shadow is to take the place of blind man. The players are allowed to dress themselves up, and disguise themselves in any way they like. Very confusing shadows may be made with a little ingenuity. The hair may be let down, or fastened up in a style different to that in which it is usually worn; or the player may wrap himself in a sheet and spread his arms wide under it, thus making a shadow like a bat; or the finger may be held over the nose to hide its shape. If the blind man looks round at the actors he must pay a forfeit for the offence.

"Schoolmaster" may be pronounced a prosaic sort of game, but it is astonishing how much amusement it is capable of affording. The players seat themselves in a circle, and one of their number, the schoolmaster, places himself before them. Pointing to the first one he says, "Tell me the name of a town beginning with such-or-such a letter," at the same time fixing upon a particular town in his own mind. If, before the schoolmaster has time to count ten in an audible whisper, the scholar can name a town beginning with that letter, he is allowed to retain his place; but if not, the question is passed on to his neighbour; and this is repeated again and again, until the town that the schoolmaster thought of is guessed. Those who can name a town "go up in class," or take the places of those who cannot do so; and if three or four players are passed, the one who succeeds at length passes them all, and each one must move a step downwards to make room for him. When the schoolmaster likes he can choose an animal, a bird, a fish, a river, a continent, a poet, a statesman, an author, or a celebrated character instead of a town.

"Russian Scandal" is a very interesting game. In this game one member of the company writes a short story on a slate, making it as full of incident as he can. He then goes outside the door, and calls one of his companions to him and reads the story aloud *once*, very distinctly. After doing this, he walks away and carries the slate with him. The person to whom the story was read summons another of the party, and narrates the story to him as exactly as he can remember

The third person tells it to a fourth, and the fourth to a fifth, and so on till each one of the party has had the story narrated to him privately and solemnly outside the door. When all have heard it, the last one to go out comes into the room and narrates the story to the whole company. The original is then read from the slate, and it is quite curious to notice how it has altered in the course of transmission. There is no necessity for any intentional inaccuracy. If only there is plenty of incident in the tale, it will be found that it is almost impossible for the person who last heard the story to repeat it exactly as the first one gave it. The little fuss that is made in entering and leaving the room makes the difficulty of remembrance all the greater.

Every one knows the excellent and lively game of "Musical Chairs." There is a variety of it, which is not so well known, called "The Huntsman." This can be played by any number above four; the more the merrier. One of the players is the huntsman, the others are named after the different parts of his dress or appurtenances. Thus there are the gun, the hat, the coat, the boots, the shot, the powder-flask, the powder, the dog, the bag, the game, &c. &c. Chairs as many as there are players, excluding the huntsman, are placed in two rows, back to back, and the players seat themselves on these. When everything is prepared, the huntsman walks round the sitters, and calls his followers by their chosen names. As each one is called he gets up and follows the huntsman. The huntsman may walk round slowly, or run, just as he likes. At any stage of the proceedings he is allowed to call out "Bang!" and immediately take possession of one of the chairs, leaving his followers to seat themselves as they can. Of course one is left out, as there is a chair less than the number of players, and that one must pay a forfeit. This game is convenient when there is not a piano in the room. When there is a piano, "Musical Chairs" played in the usual way—that is, with the players marching round the chairs to music, and scrambling for seats when the music suddenly stops—is quite as interesting.

Among twilight games, which may be played in the interval between daylight and gaslight, perhaps the best are "How, when, and where?" "What is my thought like?" or "What is it like, and why is it like it?" "Think of a word to rhyme with so-and-so;" "I apprenticed my Son;" and "Boz," or "The Game of Seven." These games are too well known to need description. As a variety, "The Spanish Merchant" may be played. The secret of this game should be known only to one or two, and the rest should try to guess it. The players take it in turns to address their next neighbour. "I'm a Spanish merchant," says one. "What do you sell?" is the retort. The secret of the game consists in the merchant being careful to name as his article of merchandise some object that he at the same time lightly and unobtru-

sively touches. If he omit to do this, the leader says, "Ah! you are no Spanish merchant," and passes on to the next. All sorts of ridiculous mistakes are made in trying to discover the mystery. "My old Grandmother doesn't like Tea" is another game of the same character. In reply to this, the question comes, "What does she like?" and the secret lies in never allowing the letter T to enter into the word which is supposed to embody the predilection of the venerable old lady.

Among the tricks which are played upon the good-natured members of a Christmas party, "Brother, I'm Bobbed," is one which excites plenty of laughter. When this is played, those who do not know the game are sent out of the room. Three chairs are then placed in the middle of the apartment, and each of the two end ones are taken possession of by a lady or gentleman. When they are comfortably seated, a large table-cloth is thrown over the heads of the couple. The players are called in, one at a time, and invited to seat themselves on the vacant chair in the middle, and the cloth is drawn over their heads also. They are then informed that they will be "bobbed" occasionally, and will be released as soon as they can guess who did the deed. The three receive in turn a knock on the head, and each one is expected to acknowledge the compliment by saying, "Brother, I'm bobbed." "Who bobbed you?" is the reply. Of course the initiated brothers inflict the blow, although they profess to suffer as much as their fellow, and the novice is inclined to charge every other member of the company with the offence before it occurs to him to accuse his companions.

A very peculiar sensation may be experienced by those who endeavour to blow out a candle without seeing where it is. The candle is lighted and placed upon a table. The player is then blindfolded, and is told to walk three steps to the right, to the left, backwards and forwards, and in each case to come back to his first position. He is then to turn round twice, and blow out the candle. In nine cases out of ten he will blow quite away from the place where the candle stands.

Perhaps it will be said that these games are not particularly new. The wise man said, "There is nothing new under the sun," and games are not the exception. The same sports which were common 150 years ago are enjoyed to-day; the only difference is that they are carried on in a more refined fashion. And it is all the pleasanter that it should be so. It is delightful to think that our children take pleasure in the same games that our grandfathers and grandmothers did. Let us hope that the Christmas season may long retain its influence, as well as its games; that it may bind heart to heart, and, as Washington Irving says, "we may draw our pleasures from the deep wells of living kindness which lie in the quiet recesses of our bosoms, and which, when resorted to, furnish forth the pure element of domestic felicity"

PHILLIS BROWNE.

HOW TO ENTERTAIN AT CHRISTMAS.

CHRISTMAS gatherings, if not entirely con-
fined to the family, are as a rule mainly
composed of relatives, possibly of all ages.
I know one happy home where four
generations have assembled for the last
three Christmas Days.

Unfortunately, family parties do not
inevitably mean concord, though they ought to do so.
There are always some lonely people whom it is a
charity to include in the invitations; and while con-
ferring a kindness, a hostess may possibly by their
presence be tending to preserve the general harmony.

The one ingredient to be universally infused is
gladness. Everybody can, at all events, *endeavour* to
bring goodwill and a smiling countenance to the
festive board, banishing for a time the recollection
of every-day worries. There is all the rest of the year

to think of them. This is peculiarly the children's
time, and we would have them as happy as we were
in the old Christmas Days of long ago.

The party may assemble only on Christmas Day,
or the house may be full from Christmas Eve until
over Twelfth Night; in both cases much depends upon
the hostess.

I think it was Lord Beaconsfield who said that
happiness was atmosphere. To bring about a general
feeling of enjoyment, much depends on the surroundings. The house must be cheerful, the ruling power
animated. It is worth while to bestow some little
trouble on the decoration of the rooms. Have plenty
of shining holly, and laurel too, and don't omit the
mistletoe, for we have long ago forgotten all about the
paganism, magic, and superstition which surrounded
it, and have relegated it to scenes of social merri-

ment. Many a shipload I have seen despatched from St. Malo, the French people hardly understanding its subsequent purpose, and a very good trade is done with it in the West of England.

I like to see a motto of welcome wrought in holly hanging in the hall, and in the yearly volume of CASSELL'S FAMILY MAGAZINE for 1877 there is an article, " How to Decorate the House at Christmas-time," with many useful suggestions. Flowers brighten up a room wonderfully, and should you have enough and to spare, I would advocate the American plan of making bells and balls of flowers to hang beneath chandeliers and over doors. They look best entirely of one kind of bloom. The balls are easily made by tying the ends with string, the bells require a founda-ion of the bell shape. Last year we made this of crinoline wire covered with coarse muslin about twelve inches long, and hid it entirely with mistletoe ; the waxen berries looked extremely pretty among the greenery as it hung over the doorway.

See that there is an abundance of Christmas litera-ture about. Servants and children as well as the grown-up guests delight in looking at pictures. A pretty, well-written story of Christmas happiness is wont to diffuse a sense of enjoyment among its readers. The glowing freshly-written pictures of the Christmas shops and the holiday people in the Christmas numbers of our magazines inspire us with a re-newed power of happiness as each season comes round.

Be sure that your hearth burns brightly. Though the yule log of Scandinavian origin is no longer drawn in by household retainers, bestridden by old Father Christmas, to be kept alight if possible to Candlemas, you will have no bad substitute in a fair-sized piece of ship's timber crackling in the grate.

It does not come within my province to enter upon the question of Christmas cheer. The board should be as liberally spread as means will allow. Children delight in a substantial tea, over which their elders can preside before their own Christmas dinner is served. An abundance of crackers and bon-bons add to the general fun—which, by-the-by, I have known enhanced by drawing lots for partners at the dinner-table.

Everybody likes presents, and presents are in-separably connected with the season. Queen Eliza-beth so delighted in them that even her "kitchen wenches" presented her with lozenges ; and fans, bracelets, and treasures of all kinds poured into the royal lap when December came.

There are two points to be considered : first, what to give, and then how best to make the giving a source of pleasure. The poor should not be forgotten. A good plan is the Christmas basket, carried pedlar fashion into the hall, and its contents distributed by all the members of the family to the poorer neighbours invited to be present, and to the servants. Such charity is doubly welcome accompanied by kindly words and wishes, and it greatly delights the young people to see their handiwork appreciated.

Christmas-trees, which the Prince Consort intro-

duced among us nearly forty years ago, have estab-lished their fame, and there is not much that is new to be told about them. They have this drawback, that in removing the presents there is a danger of fire ; and it is not a bad arrangement to hang the tree itself with beads and glittering balls brilliantly lighted, and set the presents round the table well wrapped up, a small lighted doll's-candle by each; the children are thus able to examine their gifts by the light of their very own candle. A snow-ball about a yard in circumference, made in two halves, with calico covered with wadding, on a wire foundation, filled with presents, may be rolled into the room and allowed to burst open, when a general scramble ensues. A gipsy-tent rigged up in a back drawing-room, with a presiding gipsy up to her work, who distributes the gifts with an appropriate word or two to each recipient, or a post office or parcels delivery office, with some bustling officials, may be made to produce a great deal of fun. We had a very successful distribution once from a hen's nest, con-cocted out of a clothes-basket, the gifts wrapped up to represent eggs, and the whole surmounted by a stuffed hen ; but it went off so well because we had a clever henwife, who, dressed in flowered skirts and a high pointed cap like Mother Hubbard, delighted every-body. Another year we had a Cheap Jack, who made many of us forget the pleasure our presents gave us by the roars of laughter he produced, standing in the centre of the drawing-room ottoman, and, with many a merry bon-mot, scattering the parcels here and there. The Mummers, the Lord of Misrule, St. Nicholas, or Knecht Rupert may be made to put in an appearance and give away the presents. Knecht Rupert, in Germany, makes the distribution according to the deserts of the children, dressed in a white robe, a mask, flaxen wig, and high buskins. The Lord of Misrule wears the high top-boots of Charles II.'s time, ruff at throat, and a flowing robe. He dis-appeared in 1640, but before that he presided over Christmas festivities in the houses of the king and nobles, and the Mayor of London, from Allhallow Eve to Candlemas Day. He has been resuscitated of late for the special purpose of present-giving on more than one occasion.

A Christmas ship has the advantage of being very pretty, and of exercising some ingenuity. A boy clever at carpentering could even make a good-sized one. The presents are concealed in the hold ; two feet long is a good size, and the rigging crystallised with alum to look like snow is a great improve-ment.

These distributions may take place at night or during the day, but at this season there is plenty to amuse during the day-time—long walks, when the weather is favourable, or maybe skating, and a good game of battledore and shuttlecock—or the improve-ment upon it, Badminton—in-doors, if it rains ; in which case, too, let me recommend bean-bags. For this make four bags six inches square, of strong holland, and half fill them with dry peas. The two players stand before each other, a bag in each hand, and throw simultaneously with both hands. The bag hurled from the right hand must pass to the left hand of the *vis-à-vis*, while the bag in the left hand is passed to the right, and the left hand receives the opponent's bag from his right hand. The double movement is difficult, and requires knack, but is good exercise.

If the skating-ground be near the house, some hot drinks are most acceptable, especially to those standing on the banks. I give the recipe for one which is always approved, viz., egg wine :—Beat up two eggs, and add a little cold water; boil one pint of elder wine with spice, then beat all well together, pouring from one vessel to the other, replace it on the fire till it boils, and drink when quite hot.

When the Vicar of Wakefield's altered fortunes obliged him to repair with his family to a distant neighbourhood, we read how his new parishioners "kept up the Christmas Carol, sent true love knots on Valentine's Morning, ate pancakes on Shrovetide, showed their wit on the first of April, and religiously cracked nuts on Michaelmas Eve ;" and these observances of old customs would seem to savour of a taste for simple pleasures. If carol-singing be one of them, it is certainly being revived amongst us, and this delightful form of musical amusement by young people is a Christmas pleasure worth cultivating. "God rest you, merry Gentlemen," and "Nowell, Nowell," date back to Henry VI.'s time ; "Come let us all sweet Carols sing" is of German origin ; and "We three Kings of Orient are," American ; but there are many admirable collections.

If you bring your entertainments from without, there is a choice of conjuring, a Punch and Judy show, bell-ringing, fantocinni, and the magic lantern. In the latter each year there are marked improvements, an you may follow the fortunes of Tam o' Shanter, Do Quixote, the Forty Thieves, and Johnny Gilpin, or vis the scenes of the Afghan or the Zulu War, or discove the wonders of the microscope, or enjoy the pranks o a Christmas pantomime as displayed from the lens o the white sheet.

Besides bagatelle, loto, spelicans, dominoes, and th rest, there are some newer games, such as Chines Gong, viz., a wooden stand with a pasteboard gon having a hole in the centre, into which the players throw one of six balls, which fall into numbered receptacles Patchesi, or Homeward-bound, a round game betwee draughts and fox and geese ; gobang, fishponds "How Stanley attained Congo," "Doggett's coat an badge boat-race," are amusing too, and each wee something new is brought out.

Recitations are just now very fashionable, and it i quite worth while to prepare some beforehand. D not let them be too pathetic. Shakesperian reading always please, I mean those in which each part is rea by a different person, but read carefully, and studie beforehand. A diversity of such amusement eacl evening would make a fortnight or three weeks pas all too quickly, and render the remembrance o Christmas time memorably pleasant. Recitation from good and entertaining authors never com amiss.

I cannot do better than conclude with one of the best of Christmas good wishes, which we owe to one of them : "Many merry Christmases, many happy New Years, unbroken friendships, great accumu lation of cheerful recollections, affection on earth, and heaven at last."

ARDERN HOLT.

HOW TO DECORATE THE HOUSE AT CHRISTMAS TIME.

ONG may the good old custom last of decorating our houses at Christmas. It dates back to remote ages, originating, it is said, in the Roman commemoration of the feast of Saturn. It is a symbol of our faith in the renewing power of the sun, that as the seasons return, the earth will once more be clothed with green, the trees laden with fruit. According to an old and poetical belief, the sylvan spirits flock to the evergreens in our houses, and remain unnipped by frost.

In England we depend chiefly for the greenery of our decorations on ivy, rosemary, bay laurel, box, yew, holly, and mistletoe; the bilberry playing its part sometimes. Holly is peculiarly associated with Christmas, and moreover has its own special teaching of enduring faithfulness.

> "So friends that in sunshine alone hover round,
> And when poverty threatens fly off in a volley,
> May turn to the tree that unchanging is found,
> And learn that a lesson is taught by the holly."

In decorating, one great object to be attained is uniformity, and we are inclined to think that each room should have its special feature, the heavier and more severe style being reserved for the hall and dining-room.

So great is the variety of homes in England, that it is almost impossible to furnish designs which will be applicable to all; a few general suggestions are most likely to be useful.

We will begin, then, with the hall. If the walls are bare, a lattice-work of laurel-leaves has a wonderful effect. Exact measurements should first be taken, and the foundation made in tape or strips of calico, about half an inch wide, the diamonds forming such lattice-work being all of one size. They must then be covered with laurel-leaves, each sewn on separately—a task which will furnish a few pleasant evenings' work to the younger members of the family. Should the walls be too large to cover entirely, a band of this same lattice-work just below the ceiling, and above the wainscoting, will be found very ornamental; one holly-berry, or a cluster, can be placed

at each intersection, but this is not necessary. It is a good plan when each strip is finished to wrap it in a damp cloth and place it in the cellar; and this should be done to all garlands, wreaths, &c., not immediately required.

Facing the doorway, or in as conspicuous a place as possible, there should be a motto either of welcome or one appropriate to the season, such as "A Merry Christmas and a Happy New Year," with the crest and monogram of the family on either side.

"A Happy Christmas.".

"Christmas Greetings."

"A Hundred Thousand Welcomes."
Shakespeare, *Coriolanus*, Act II., Scene 1.

"You are very Welcome to our House."
Merchant of Venice, Act V., Scene 1.

"Then let us all rejoice amain on Christmas Day."

"Kind hearts can make December blithe as May,
And in each morrow find a New Year's Day."

"Welcome be ye good New Year;
Welcome be ye that are here;
Welcome all and make good cheer—
Welcome all another year."

The latter three are somewhat lengthy, but each line of the last of all, which is taken from the Sloane Manuscripts of Henry VI.'s time, might be used by itself. These and other mottoes can be carried out in various ways. We will enumerate a few.

A slight wooden framework covered with Turkey-red, either paper or calico; a bordering of holly or laurel-leaves round; the lettering laid on in green leaves or white paper, or imitation ivory, produced by cutting the letters in cardboard, which cover with gum tragacanth, and then sprinkle with either raw rice or tapioca. The grains must lie quite close together, placed in successive layers, allowing each to dry before another is added, half an inch being about the necessary depth. If varnished over with red sealing-wax dissolved in spirits of wine, this has the effect of coral, and should be put on a white ground.

Letters in white cotton-wool have a very snow-like effect, which is enhanced if they are slightly damped with starch-water, and then sprinkled with frosting powder. Be careful in cutting the wool to have the smooth side uppermost, using it the reverse way. Instead of a bordering of leaves round the framework, icicles may be substituted, made of cotton-wool pulled into form, and sprinkled in the same manner; a blue background being substituted for red, if preferred.

A hall should have plenty of light in it, therefore when evening closes in such decorations sparkle and glisten, and on this account alum letters are to be recommended. They are formed in wire wrapped in worsted. The alum is prepared by dissolving it in as much water as it will take up, pour this into an earthen vessel and boil it down to half; strain it, let it come to the boil again, and suspend the letters in it, setting it for awhile in a cool place. The result will be that the worsted becomes one mass of pure white crystals. Sulphate of copper with the alum will make them blue ; yellow prussiate of potass, yellow ; red prussiate of potass, ruby.

Letters in holly-berries on a white ground are Christmas-like, and peas dipped in a solution of red sealing-wax are admirable substitutes for berries where they run short. The blooms of coloured everlasting flowers, close-set, have by no means a bad effect, but

Letters made of brown paper, rolled and flattened into the form required, then gummed and covered with tin foil, are a novelty ; if this is well crumpled first, it resembles frosted silver. Cardboard, straw, or zinc letters, some of the latter perforated so that anything can be sewn to them, may be purchased ready for use, and considerably lighten the labour of decorating.

The mistletoe-bough must not be forgotten—that well-known plant sacred to the goddess of beauty, which the old Druids fetched from the woods with so

they are rather too ecclesiastical for house decorations. We have, however, seen them used with a pin stuck in each blossom, showing the head, and giving a silvery hue.

Permanent mottoes are not to be despised, as they can be stored away and used for successive years. Illuminated lettering, and gold and coloured paper letters pasted on a white ground, come under this head. Ears of corn on red and blue backgrounds make effective letters, as are those in the well-known paper rosette work, which requires a red or blue velvet background. A simple plan for paper letters is to cover the design of the words with paper florets, made by cutting rounds of tissue paper the size of half-a-crown, sewing five one inside the other, creasing them together, and setting them closely side by side.

much ceremony, their followers adorning their dwellings therewith, as an emblem of good fortune.

According to the old superstition, the maiden who escapes kissing beneath it at Christmas time has no hope of marrying within the year.

The mistletoe, then, should be suspended from the centre chandelier, or in some prominent part of the hall ; but where it is not to be had, we must fall back, as did our ancestors, on the so-called kissing-bough, made of evergreens tied with coloured ribbons, having oranges depending.

Garlands round pillars, up staircases, and suspended from each corner of a room or hall to the centre, will repay the trouble of making. For entwining, flat wreaths are best, and these should be made by sewing the leaves in pairs or trios on a strip of green calico, with holly-berries down the centre if preferred.

Holly-leaves, each separately threaded in the centre on coarse black cotton, make a handsome garland, which shows best round antlers or clocks, or about an oval glass. Garlands all round alike are best made on soft cord, or what is called "bag strapping," cut the length required, always remembering that it will pretty certainly take up in using. Wind the evergreens in small pieces round this centre cord with string. Coloured glass balls attached at intervals, and Chinese lanterns, are a vast improvement where the room will admit of them.

Archways and doorways should not be left unadorned. For these, measure the exact size, and cut a strip of calico the length. The middle of this is for the centre of the doorway or archway; ornament it with a large rosette of leaves and holly, intermixed if you like with some of the many coloured and white grasses and Cape flowers now to be had, and of an exquisite feathery appearance. Similar rosettes, only smaller, should be placed in the centre of the strip on either side, with rows of leaves sewn on flat between.

If you wish to make the holly look snow-laden, moisten it with weak gum, or starch-water, and then sprinkle with flour from a dredger.

All these garlands and mottoes may be introduced with good effect in dining-rooms, billiard-rooms, and corridors.

Flowers in the winter are luxuries, but narcissus, lilies, stephanotis, primulas, camelias, hyacinths, geraniums, &c., are to be had, and a great effect may be produced by making beds of moss in quiet nooks, and round the foot of staircases, into which pots of flowers in bloom, or cut flowers, may be plunged. Cut ferns are invaluable in decorations. If pressed between blotting-paper when gathered, then saturated with green dye, and pressed again, they will last almost any time.

Drawing-rooms and boudoirs may be decorated in a less cumbersome and heavy style, although we would not entirely banish holly; small sprays let into the perforated interstices of gold frames, china mirrors, &c., are exceedingly pretty.

The fields are rich in summer and autumn with exquisite grasses of endless variety, which only required to be gathered. They dry in any vase without special care, and these will mingle well with flowers at Christmas time. We have used them with dried bulrushes over the doorways, which we thus converted into a sort of bower, with stuffed birds hovering in the midst.

Feather mottoes have a good effect in boudoirs and drawing-rooms, and although pheasants and foreign birds have more brilliant plumage, the poultry yard will furnish a good supply—none more beautiful than the soft marabout feathers found beneath the wing of the white turkey. These on a blue ground form an exquisite symbol of snow, conveying Christmas greetings. Industrious fingers have a wide field of usefulness, and letters worked in point-lace united by twisted threads, or crocheted in white wool with a bright background, would be by no means the least attractive of house decorations at Christmas time.

CHRISTMAS VERSES.

I.—CHRISTMAS SIGNS.

THE wind sighs leafless trees among,
The fire burns bright, the nights are long,
The robin sings his winter song,
   And the Christmas snow is falling.

Frost crystals lend their shining light
To rubies from the holly bright,
And mistletoe's pure pearls of white,
   When the Christmas snow is falling.

To those that smile, and those that weep,
Come peaceful visions as they sleep ;
For Christmas angels vigil keep,
   When the Christmas snow is falling.

Age thinks of many a Christmas past,
And hears old stories in the blast
Of Christmas Days too bright to last,
   When the Christmas snow is falling.

While youth but learns from that same breeze
Of countless Christmas Days like these,
And glorious golden prospects sees,
   When the Christmas snow is falling.

II.—THE CHRISTMAS-TREE.

A FLASH of light, a merry hum,
   And peals of rippling laughter sweet,
   The pattering of tiny feet,
And, lo, the little children come.

A stately fir-tree rears its head,
   With stars and tapers all a-blaze ;
   And quivering in the fairy rays,
The glittering, loaded branches spread.

And childish eyes are sparkling bright,
   And childish hearts with joy o'erflow,
   And on that Birth-day long ago
They ponder with a grave delight.

Then to their gifts they turn once more,
   And in the present sunshine lost,
   They fear no future tempest-tossed,
But unto fairy regions soar.

No cares, no fears, a happy time
   Of laughter ; tears that cannot stay ;
   An April day, a year of May,
Pealed in and out with Christmas chime.

III.—THE MISTLETOE.

SWIFTLY time is onward stealing,
Christmas revelries revealing ;
And the mistletoe is showing
Pearls more precious than are glowing
In the depths of Persian waters ;
For old England's blooming daughters,
Blushing, slily smiling, know
Magic lies in mistletoe.

Many a secret sweet reposes
Underneath the moss-veiled roses ;
But the mistletoe hath folden
Hearts within its branches olden,
And no plant so sweet as this is,
With its wealth of Christmas kisses ;
Youth and maiden come to know,
Magic lies in mistletoe.

Many a Christmas coming, going,
With its festal joys o'erflowing,
Sees the mistletoe still reigning
And its subjects soft enchaining ;
Many a sad heart making lighter,
Many a merry one the brighter,
Through the magic that men know
Lies in white-gemmed mistletoe.

IV.—WASSAIL.

UPRAISE the Christmas bowl to-night
  And let a health go round;
To those we love in every land,
To those who 'neath our roof-tree stand,
  May Christmas joys abound.

To those that love us, joy and peace,
  Whether afar or near;
To old and young, to rich and poor,
Be merry Christmas Days in store,
  And hope in the New Year.

Ay, even to our foes we drink,
  And what the worse are we?
For if they hate, and we forgive,
'Tis ours the sweeter life to live,
  Whilst theirs shall bitter be.

Upraise the bowl—we toast the last,
  The one we love the best,
Whose love hath made our life to shine—
Turned earth to Paradise divine,
  The work-day world to rest.

Upraise the Christmas bowl to-night,
  And may each Christmas Day
Be hostel-sign where we may meet
All lovingly home-friends to greet,
  And pledge those far away.

V.—IN THE SILVER AGE.

ROUND the fire the gossips sit,
  Telling many an ancient story;
Memory wreathes their brows to-night
  With a golden Christmas glory.

Soft, like honey-dew, there flows
  From their lips long stored-up treasures,
Of the days when they and Time
  Ran a race in spring-tide pleasures.

Gently, rev'rently they speak,
  Smilingly, yet nigh to weeping,
Of the fair transfigured past
  Still a present with them keeping:

Tell of Christmas kisses felt,
  E'en to-night, although the giver
Lies beneath the Christmas snow.
  Out beyond the darksome river.

This one fell on battle-field,
  That one sleeps beneath the billow,
And another faded, though
  Loving hands had smoothed his pillow.

Up they rise at Memory's call,
  All the lost familiar faces:
Who shall speak the words they spake,
  Who shall stand in their old places?

Hush! no grief or care for them—
  Hark! the Christmas angels calling,
Peace to us and peace to them,
  When the Christmas snow is falling.

VI.—AMEN!

HUSH! the Christmas Day is ending,
Angels on the earth descending
  Bless the world to-night.
Glory streameth down from heaven,
Peace unto mankind is given
  Through the Light
That came down from heaven above,
Lighting all the world through Love.
      Amen!
          JULIA GODDARD.

CHILDREN'S FANCY DRESS FOR CHRISTMAS PARTIES.

"JILL."

FANCY costumes are particularly well adapted to little folks, a fact which of late years has come to be recognised, and at many juvenile parties character costumes are *de rigueur*. In case any of my readers should receive invitations to such parties for the young members of their family, and be puzzled how to dress them, I propose to give some details that I trust may be acceptable, and shall begin with those which are particularly easy to make at home. Boys' costumes, as a rule, not being so easy as girls', I will discuss the boys' first.

Geneviève de Brabant gave prominence to a cook's dress, and nothing is easier—and I was going to say quainter. It must be all white, even to shoes and cotton stockings ; the breeches are made of white linen, and fastened with three buttons at the knee, and over this is either a frilled blouse, full, and ending at the waist, or a white double-breasted tail-coat ; the white apron must, *de rigueur*, be tucked into the waist, and the flat cook's cap be worn on the head. If you want any further decoration, you may wear the *cordon bleu*, display a bill of fare, or a sauce-pan ; and should you prefer to be a pastrycook, you carry a wooden tray of cakes ; or a baker, you carry a long Vienna loaf.

A clown — more especially the

FRENCH DRESS, 1787.

French one, Pierrot—is very easily concocted. He wears long, loose, white trousers and blouse, with a row of coloured rosettes down the front, and has his face painted, and occasionally has a half-mask, black. An æsthetic clown is a good notion, with sunflowers and blue china plates worked over the white dress, a peacock's feather in the conical cap, a sunflower and a feather-fan carried in the hand.

A wizard, or astrologer, is easily managed : a black conical cap, with cabalistic insignia pasted on in gold paper, and a long black robe with the same, a wand in the hand, large spectacles, a ruff at the throat, made of treble box-plaited muslin, and pointed shoes.

Mirliton is a pretty dress for a boy, and of much the same cut as the clown's, only that the blouse is more close-fitting, but pointed cap, blouse, and rousers should be covered with inch-wide stripes of blue cotton, stitched on diagonally, so that they appear to be wound round and round.

A Christy minstrel, in striped linen coat and trousers, preposterously large collar, a black face, and a battered hat, is capital for a big boy, as some little fun can be brought to bear on the character.

Small boys dressed as Napoleon the Great, Dr. Pangloss, a jockey, Dick Turpin, and other well-known characters are irresistibly charming. As I have mentioned these, and you might select them, I must tell you how to dress them. Napoleon I. has a black cocked hat, with tricolour rosette, a large lapelled coat, white leather breeches, silk stockings, and shoes. Dr. Pangloss, a large-skirted, large-sleeved black velvet coat, with steel buttons, a very long waistcoat, black velvet breeches, ruffles, shoes with buckles, white wig, and spectacles. A jockey appears in a parti-coloured jacket and breeches of satin, cap to match, top-boots, a whip in hand. Dick Turpin, in a scarlet coat and waistcoat trimmed with gold braid and buttons, lace ruffles and cravat, leather breeches, high boots, and three-cornered hat and fancy wig, with pistols at the belt. I consider that the most

LADY OF THE TWELFTH CENTURY.

FISHWIFE.

A PAGE.

all of a row" on her pink and blue gown; a châtelaine formed of watering-pot, hoe, rake, and spade at her side. Red Riding Hood, in red cloak and blue frock, was there, as well as Chaperon Rouge, the French and more dainty rendering of the same, viz., a red satin petticoat, black velvet bodice, white muslin apron, and red silk hood, a basket in the hand; and also Cinderella, both as a princess and a serving-maid, but in both cases displaying her crystal shoe — by-the-by, best made by covering a discarded white satin shoe with talc cloth. There were several other characters.

favourite fancy costume for boys just now is the man-of-war's man, because everybody has a sailor suit; and the æsthetic costume, which is rendered by black pointed shoes, silk stockings, light velvet breeches, short jacket, and a large soft coat. An æsthetic green is really the colour that should be chosen, but a black velvet is as often as not adopted, and that can be worn afterwards in every-day life.

Any characters from the nursery rhymes and stories seem well adapted to children, and at one of the prettiest juvenile parties I have seen, no other costumes were admitted. Jack Horner in blue breeches and waistcoat, a red coat with gold buttons, a tricolour hat, and a plum hanging to his watch-chain, dragged by the hand the very smallest brother, who personated Jack the valiant Giant Killer. The little fellow in his blue trunk-hose, close-fitting red habit, helmet, shield, and sword, seemed to have come direct from the kingdom of Liliputia. Boy Blue as Gainsborough painted him; Blue Beard with a thick beard of blue wool; Beauty and the Beast devoted themselves to "My pretty Maid," in a quilted petticoat, bunched-up chintz tunic, muslin kerchief, straw hat, and milk-pails; and to "Mary, Mary, quite Contrary," who had "cockle shells, silver bells, and pretty girls,

Kate Greenaway's heroines suit little people wonderfully well, and you can hardly do wrong in copying her illustrations faithfully. I have in my mind's eye a little damsel of eight years old, with auburn hair and sparkling eyes, who as Jennie won all hearts. She was not, as I have seen the character rendered, in black silk dress, muslin apron, kerchief and cap—captivating enough when a bright young face peeps from beneath—but in a short green skirt and pelisse, with poke bonnet and fur muff, a lace pelerine over her shoulders, and high-heeled shoes. Quaker's and quiet dresses, which elderly people might wear, are always piquant on a child, just as the garb of a baby or of a schoolboy is extremely amusing worn by a grown man. Vandyck's famous picture of Charles I.'s children may always serve as a guide to a family group. The close lace cap, the long skirt, the bibbed apron suit little girls to perfection, and there is hardly a picture which Vandyck, Sir Joshua Reynolds, Gainsborough, or De Largillière painted of children which would not show to advantage if reproduced at a juvenile fancy ball.

MOORISH SERVANT.

FORESTER.

If you wish to make a boy thoroughly happy, let him appear as Robinson Crusoe in knickerbockers and paletot and cap of fur, with robins sewn about it, a parrot perched on the shoulder, a belt round the waist, carrying a fowling-piece, pistols, hatchet, and umbrella; and a little friend should be allowed to accompany him as Man Friday with blacked face and hands and feet, wearing a striped shirt and trousers. Lalla Rookh and other Eastern dresses suit dark girls well. If I describe Lalla Rookh I shall be describing the ordinary run of Oriental dresses. She has full red silk trousers to the ankle, a short petticoat to match, a green satin over-dress with open sleeves trimmed with gold, a pink satin bodice over a gold-spangled chemisette. A few illustrations will make this paper of more practical use; they are as follows:—

BARRISTER.

No. 1. *Jill.*—In a flowered cotton frock and petticoat; soft silk kerchief, knotted at the throat. The large brim of the bonnet should be lined with a colour becoming to the wearer.

No. 2. *French Dress about* 1787.—Pale blue and yellow striped silk coat; yellow satin breeches; long blue waistcoat, fastening to the waist, then opening to disclose a blue under-vest trimmed with gold braid. Chain and seals hanging at the side. Large lace jabot in front, and lace ruffles at the wrists. White wig; tricornered black hat; gold-headed cane.

No. 3. *Lady of the Twelfth Century.*—Dark woollen dress, with three-inch border of contrasting colour; the long sleeves match the border, likewise the pointed

fichu in front. Velvet collar. The pointed head-dress is white and gold; the veil is white; a velvet band borders the edge, and lace frills fall on the hair. Gold ornaments, pointed shoes.

No. 4. *Fishwife.*—Woollen dress, either dark blue or dark terra-cotta red; soft silk pink kerchief for the head. Stockings striped to match dress.

No. 5. *Forester.*—Dark woollen tights, hood, and hose. Boots, belt, jacket, and gauntlets of soft leather. Felt hat; staff in hand.

No. 6. *Page.*—Tights and vest joined by ribbons, and showing a soft shirt at the neck, waist, and wrists. Hanging sleeves lined with a contrasting colour falling over close ones. Long hair and round hat.

No. 7. *Moorish Servant.*— Striped silk trousers; embroidered satin jacket; Oriental scarf round hips; soft muslin turban. The hands and face should be stained.

No. 8. *Barrister.* — Black gown, either in black lustre or rich corded silk; scarf in either black or crimson silk; wig; brief in hand.

No. 9. *Dutch Woman.*—Short-waisted dress, with square velvet-trimmed bodice; gauntlet sleeves

DUTCH WOMAN.

with a puff of cambric at the elbow; elaborately gathered chemisette; lawn apron with handsome lace border.

In fancy costumes everything depends on brightness of colour, freshness, and suitability. Nervous children should not be put into dresses which are associated with a marked bearing or the quiet self-possession of a woman of the world; they can hardly help looking well whatever they wear, so let them have all the enjoyment they can.

The Friendly Visitor

MOTHER'S CHRISTMAS PRESENT.

By Hetty Procter.

"MOTHER, next Friday is Christmas Day. Will you make us a plum-pudding?"

"And get some holly?"

"Mother, say you will."

Mrs. Jennings sighed as she gazed at the eager little speakers. "I am sorry to disappoint you, dears," she said, gently; "but I am afraid you will have to do without holly and plum-pudding this year."

"Oh, mother, we always had one

before; and I am so tired of bread, and the nasty dinners we have."

"Hush, Willie! you must be thankful I can get bread for you."

"But, mother, are we so poor that we can't even have a pudding for Christmas?"

"Yes, Netta. You know that during the strike we spent all the money we had saved, and got into debt besides. And now the landlord says if we don't pay all the rent we owe by the new year, we must leave."

"Never mind, movver," said little Bell, suddenly; "if you can't buy us some 'Kismas,' we will buy you some. I've got a penny."

The other children shouted with laughter, and Harry exclaimed, "You little muff! A penny won't buy nothing but toffee or an orange. It takes pounds to buy plum-pudding and things."

Bell began to cry. "Never mind, dearie," said Mrs. Jennings, kissing her fondly; "mother is as pleased as if you had given her the best Christmas dinner that could be bought. Now run and play; I have this work to finish."

Tom Jennings was a clever workman, and being a sober, steady fellow, usually earned good wages; but owing to a strike, he had been out of work for weeks. During that time they had lived upon their savings, and on what Mrs. Jennings could earn. She had obtained some coarse shirts to make, but was not very well paid for them. The strike was over now, yet it would take them a long time to regain their former comfortable position.

"I say it is a shame!" cried Harry, that evening when the children were alone, "not to have even a pudding."

"So do I," said Willie; "and when I am a man I won't go on strike."

"Greedy things!" Netta exclaimed; "you think of nobody but yourselves."

"Well, father shouldn't have gone on strike."

"But father didn't want to go on strike," retorted Netta, "and I know he feels it like anything disappointing us, and I saw mother crying this afternoon after you had been asking about Christmas."

Willie looked uncomfortable, and shuffled uneasily. Netta continued, "Don't you think it would be nice if we could give them a Christmas dinner this year, instead of them giving us one?"

The magnitude of this proposal quite took away the breath of the boys, and for a moment they could only stare at Netta.

"But how can we?" gasped Harry, at length; "we have no money."

"I know that, stupid! We must earn it," answered Netta, briskly. "You boys must sweep the snow away for people and hold horses, and I will run errands and mind babies. Next week will be the holidays, so we shall have plenty of time."

The boys had a great respect for Netta, and when their first astonishment was over, they entered into her plans with great enthusiasm. It was decided that Bell should try to sell the pretty things she made at the kindergarten, and that their scheme was to be kept a profound secret.

For the next few days Mrs. Jennings could not think what had come to the children. They rose up early in the mornings, and were out all day in spite of the cold and snow. It was fortunate for the keeping of the secret that a larger order than usual kept her very busy, or she must have guessed. As it was, when Bell chattered about what she would buy for mother's "Kismas," she only smiled.

Christmas Eve came at last. The children had prospered in their work, and had decided that at tea-time the money should be given to their mother. How quickly the bread and weak tea were despatched! There was no grumbling to-night! As soon as the last crumb had vanished, Netta produced a bag.

"See, mother," she said, " this is a Christmas present for you."

"To buy Christmas pudding and holly and things," shouted the boys.

Wonderingly, Mrs. Jennings looked into the bag. "Children, children, where did you get all this money from?" she cried.

"We earned it, mother," said Netta, proudly; and taking the bag, she emptied the contents into her mother's lap.

"Bless you all!" cried their mother, proudly. "How hard you must have worked! Why, there is ten shillings and fivepence!"

Mr. Jennings came in at this moment, and the wonderful news was told to him. He decreed that every penny should be spent on Christmas cheer. Everybody must help to spend that money, of course.

So by-and-by a happy little party started out. The well-worn basket grew heavy, and the old purse light, before the marketing was done; but at length the purchases were all made, and the party turned homewards.

Passing a brilliantly-lighted house, in one of the windows they saw a beautiful Christmas-tree, and gaily dressed children dancing round it. They all stopped to look at the pretty sight.

"I wish we had a Christmas-tree," sighed Willie.

"My boy, learn to be contented," said his mother. "You have made me so happy to-day, don't grumble now."

Willie's face cleared, and the blind being drawn down at this moment, they hastened home.

What a happy Christmas Day that was! As they all sat round the fire roasting chestnuts, Mrs. Jennings declared she had never enjoyed a Christmas Day so much; and, though they had no Christmas-tree, the children agreed that they had never been so happy before.

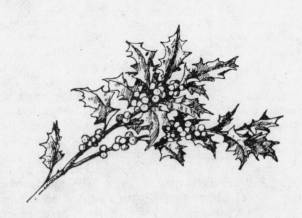

STEPHEN CLARKE'S CHRISTMAS CAROL.

IT was Christmas Day, and Stephen Clarke sat in his accustomed corner of the old church of Stretfield. He was the churchwarden, and the most highly-respected man in the whole parish. Everyone had a good word for Stephen, who was a bachelor, and lived alone in a cosy little cottage close to the church. His brother Philip—a good-for-nothing fellow, who had quarrelled with Stephen when they were both young—lived at the other end of the village, with his sickly wife and his two little girls, Mattie and Molly. Stephen had made up the quarrel long ago, but he did not care to see much of poor Philip, who was no credit to anyone, and certainly not a relation to be proud of. Stephen loved the old church, and was never so happy as when he was inside its walls ; and as he sat there that Christmas morning— hale and strong and well-to-do, and harassed by no cares of wife or children —there was no more contented man in Stretfield than Stephen Clarke. Poor Mattie and Molly sat near to him. The children were alone, as Philip had not been inside a church for years, and his hard-working wife maintained that she had no time to come and no fit clothes to come in ; and as Stephen looked at the wistful little faces, he felt glad that, beyond his handsome annual present to them, he was not troubled with unfortunate Philip and his delicate wife and children.

The church felt very warm and comfortable on coming in out of the sharp, frosty air, and Stephen Clarke was becoming conscious of a pleasant drowsiness, when suddenly he was surprised to see that the chancel was filled with a choir of white-robed angels, instead of with the ordinary surpliced schoolchildren ; and as for the music, it was far more beautiful than anything he had ever heard in his life before.

" *Glory to God in the highest, and on earth peace, good will toward men.*"

So sang the angel-chorus, and the wonderful strains seemed to lift the arching roof, and to ascend right up to heaven.

Stephen felt that he must join in this glorious Christmas carol, so he also raised his voice, as was his wont in the house of God. But, alas ! great was his surprise and horror to hear himself singing—

" *Glory to Stephen Clarke, and on earth ease, disdain toward men.*"

The angels all looked round to see what mortal had thus dared to mar their heavenly melody, and poor Stephen was ready to sink through the floor for very shame and confusion. He could not imagine what possessed him to do such a thing, as he had intended to sing the same words that the angels were singing. Then he perceived that one of the choir was standing beside him, and whilst he gazed in silent awe, the angel said—

" What doest thou here, Stephen ? The song that thou art singing is not fit for angel-ears."

" Oh, sir," cried Stephen, in anguish, " pray tell me why such words came out of my lips. Why cannot I sing your Christmas carol ? "

" Because thou hast not learned it, Stephen. *Glory to God* has never been thy theme."

Clarke regarded the angel with amazement.

" Pardon me, sir," he said, " but how can you say that of me, who have devoted myself to the work of the church and the good of the parish from my youth up until now ? "

The angel smiled.

" True," he answered, " thou hast graced the fold and guarded the flock, but thou didst it in order that men might speak well of thee and praise thee ; and thou hast gained the desire of thine heart, for there is no man in Stretfield more beloved and respected than thyself. *Glory to Stephen Clarke* has been the theme of thy life, as it is the theme of thy carol this Christmas Day ; but it is not a song that angels care to hear."

Then Stephen's heart was heavy within him, for he felt the truth of every word that his companion uttered, and he knew that the calm angel-eyes were piercing his very soul. After a moment he spoke again :

" But pray tell me, great angel, why I likewise fail to sing aright the second part of the heavenly carol. I have ever been a peace-loving man, and to no living creature do I bear ill-will."

" It is *ease* that thou hast sought, not

eace," answered the angel; "thou hast not loved thy fellow-men enough for their doings to trouble thee."

"But I have given alms," said Stephen.

"To be seen of men," replied the angel.

"And I made friends with my brother Philip, though I am sure his was the fault, not mine."

"And thou didst let him alone," continued the angel, "because he was no credit to thee; and thou didst quieten thy conscience by a yearly gift to him out of thine abundance; and thou wert thankful that his sickly wife and children did not disturb the comfort of thy soul. Such doings earn the praise of men, Stephen; but they are far from the glory of God. As thou hast lived, so must thou sing; and thy singing is not such as angels love to listen to."

Then Stephen was humbled to the dust before the angel; and as he was pondering in his heart what to say in order to appease the righteous wrath of his stern accuser, he opened his eyes, and behold! it was all a dream. He was sitting in his usual corner of the church, the surpliced choir-boys were singing in their stalls, and Mattie and Molly's thin little voices were joining in the Christmas carol.

But though the dream passed away, its influence abode with Stephen Clarke, urging him to translate into practical realisation the lesson he had been taught. When the service was over, he joined the two little girls, to their great surprise, and walked home with them. His brother looked up in amazement as Stephen entered the poverty-stricken dwelling, and it was indeed awkward for the long-estranged churchwarden to explain the change which had come over him. But at length he succeeded, and presently, by a little loving persuasion, he brought back Philip and Philip's wife and children, and made them sit down with him to his comfortable Christmas dinner in his cosy cottage.

Stephen Clarke never forgot that wonderful dream of his. He made up his mind that for the future he would seek the praise of God rather than the praise of men; and would strive to regard his neighbour, not with the easy tolerance of a selfish indifference, but with the love that "beareth all things, believeth all things, hopeth all things, endureth all things." He and his brother renewed the boyish affection of bygone days; and with Stephen at his side to guide and encourage him, Philip became quite a respectable member of society. The careworn wife grew brighter and stronger in these happier circumstances; while Mattie and Molly were the light of their uncle's eyes and the joy of his old age.

On the next Christmas Day, when Stephen Clarke stood up in his old corner of the church, surrounded by his brother and his brother's family, he felt that now he might sing from his heart—

"*Glory to God in the highest, and on earth peace, good will toward men.*"

And this time his carol was one that angels loved to listen to.

ELLEN THORNEYCROFT FOWLER.

ONE CHRISTMAS EVE.

EOPLE called them "Ruth and Naomi"—young Mrs. Towner and "Gran." The brave, busy young dressmaker, who went to "gentlefolks'" houses to earn what she could by her needle, had refused to part from her husband's mother, even though the news had come that he had died of fever abroad, and nothing but her own earnings kept the old lady from the workhouse.

"Gran," said little Joe, drawing pictures by the fire on Christmas Eve, and dreaming of the kind of Christmas it might have been, "I saw the soldiers marching in from the docks to-day, and everyone cheered them. Won't their folks be happy this Christmas, Gran?"

"Ay, laddie, dear, they'll be thankful and happy to see their own again."

"I wish daddy had come home with the rest, Gran. Why didn't God keep him alive, and let him come home with pretty medals, and make mother and all of us glad? Why did God let daddy go and die across the sea, Gran?"

"Josie, *He* knows why. I've lived to the time of grey hairs, laddie, and I've learnt this: to keep on asking '*why*' is heart-breaking work; but it's a heart-rest to believe our God and Father chooses the very best, the very tenderest for us all, and He *knows* the reason why things happen that seem to go wrong. We shall know the reason too one day, Josie."

"I wish daddy hadn't died across the sea though, Gran, with none of us to say good-bye to him. It seems so dreadful to think he died alone."

"Not alone, my laddie, for He who sees the little sparrows fall forgets not our dear ones in their last hour. And why should we say good-bye? There's a Golden Land, my dearie, where we are all going to meet in the Morning."

"Charlie Benson's father is a sergeant," said Joe, rather wistfully, "and they're going to have a big pudding

"'Our Father chooses the very best for us all.'"

or Christmas, and nuts, and crackers, and figs, and almonds, and raisins. And his father's going to give him a bright shilling. Gran, we're dreadful poor, aren't we? Nobody ever gives us anything."

" Dearie, we are rich in each other's love and in the love of the Holy One, born for us a little Child. Ours is a glorious Christmas Gift, dearie, a gift that the poorest may possess. Shall we not bless and praise God, even though bread alone be our Christmas fare?"

And she carefully cut the loaf and began to make some toast for her daughter-in-law's supper. She was a little anxious about Josie's mother. The church clock near had struck nine, and the chimes were ringing, as they always did at nine,—

"Abide with me; fast falls the eventide."

" There's something coming bump, bump, bump upstairs," said Josie.

Sure enough, the "bump" stopped at their door. Josie opened the door, but it took the two of them to drag in the hamper that stood outside.

Joe's little mouth watered as he saw mince-pies, a ham, oranges, a plum-pudding in a basin, a sugared cake, a huge loaf, butter, tea, sugar, and cocoa.

"It is a mistake," said "Gran"; ' these things are not for us."

But Josie's mother came quietly in and took her wrinkled hands in her own, and the old lady's eyes grew moist with happy tears like hers.

"Mother," she said, softly, "there was One born at Christmas Who knows a mother's heart. And when the widow mourned for her son as dead, the Lord Jesus brought him back to life and gave him to his mother."

"Gran" looked earnestly into the sweet young face.

"This, my son," she faltered, "was dead, and is alive again."

"Yes, mother," said a familiar voice, and three seemed clasped at once in the soldier's arms. "The rumour of my death was false. I have been discharged invalided, with a good record, thank the Lord! I have a pension, and because I helped to save his life, my former major is going to get me employment as timekeeper in some works owned by his brother. Brighter times are dawning for us all, mother, and I sent in this hamper as an earnest of good things yet in store. Happy Christmas to everyone, and no more tears; they're not Christmassy. Let's try a carol instead."

But his own voice broke down as he began, for he had never thought to see those dear faces again. Nobody could sing, save in their hearts, except little Joe, and he voiced the feelings of all by starting a piece he had learnt at school:

" Roll on, roll on the tide of praise,
  Faint hearts break out in singing !
Lift up your heads, rejoice, rejoice,—
  The Christmas bells are ringing ! "

M. S. HAYCRAFT.

If Sinners Entice thee ◉ Consent thou Not.

PROVERBS I-10

Be ye followers of GOD as dear Children.

EPH·V·I

CHRISTMAS.

ONCE more we hail the welcome day
   Which brings to mind the Saviour's birth ;
Let festal joys drive gloom away,
   Let peace encircle all the earth,
While we with gladness celebrate
The birth of our Great Potentate.

From Him we learn the law of love
   And how we may our blessings share ;
By active sympathy we prove
   That we for one another care ;
Thus all in kindest deeds unite
To fill the season with delight.

Not for that light which brightly shone,
   Nor music sweet as angel's song,
But for the King Himself alone
   Our waiting spirits watch and long :
His birth we gladly celebrate,
And for His second coming wait.

One day of Christmas joys, and then
   The world its common course pursues,
Unmindful of the morning when
   The angels brought the joyful news ;
But when the King Himself appears
The joy will last through endless years.

T. WATSON.

A CHRISTMAS HYMN.

WHILE far and wide this joyful day
   The snow in silence falls,
With Christmas mirth our homes are gay,
   And green boughs deck the walls.

Though wintry blasts rave loud and keen
   Across the landscape white,
What looks of happiness are seen
   By firesides gleaming bright !

It is the day of all the year
   When, from the belfries round,
The pealing chimes we love to hear
   Awake in sweetest sound !

The angels' anthem we recall,
   The tidings told to them
Who worshipped in the lowly stall
   The Babe of Bethlehem !

Thou Light of Light, whose beams abound
   To pierce our deepest gloom,
Though in the inn no room was found,
   Our hearts would make Thee room !

Accept our praises, Lord, again
   Upon this blissful morn,
With peace on earth, good will to men,
   Henceforth in beauty born !

J. R. EASTWOOD.

CABBY'S CHRISTMAS SURPRISE.

By M. S. Haycraft, Author of "Under the Blossom," etc.

"HAD a good day, Jim?"
"*All* days are good, Bessie, my girl."

"You'll never look on naught but the bright side, Jim," said his wife, helping him off with his coat; "and you're right enough, for every day that

comes brings us goodness and mercy from our Lord."

"Have lots of people been riding in the cab to-day, daddy?" asked six-year-old Nelly, climbing on the cabman's knee.

"Not one, my lassie. Daddy's taken ne'er a fare to-day."

"Not one? You don't mean it, Jim, and money going out of your pocket each week to Mr. Wilson for the cab."

"I've never known it so afore, Bessie," he said to his wife. "Ain't that something to be thankful for now, that I can't remember a day—not for years—when I've taken not a sixpence, and I don't suppose it's likely to happen again either."

"That's bad," said his wife, her face clouding as she thought of Christmas drawing near and very little to spare to make cheer for the children. "I suppose as it's so cold folks won't be riding if they've got time to walk. You'll be busier next week, Jim, when the boys and girls come home from boarding-school; but it's unfortunate, for Jessie's bronchitis run away with a good lot of money, and we're getting a bit low; we'll have to be very careful."

"Never mind, old girl. Jessie's pulled through fine now, haven't you, my lass?" said Barton to his elder girl, as he stroked her hair; "and the money's better spent for milk and eggs and things like that than for beer and spirits. We haven't *wasted* it, that's a blessing."

"But you're so late this evening, Jim, that says I to myself, 'He's got a good fare, and he'll be coming in with rare good news to-night.'"

"Yes, I'm a bit late, my girl, but I took old Jack to the stables a good while ago, and, upon my word, the old chap rubbed his head against me, as much as to say, 'Don't be downhearted, Barton, old fellow! There'll be lots of folks wanting a lift in the cab to-morrow.'"

"Old Jack knows," said Jessie, nodding her curly head; "old Jack's as clever as if he could talk."

"He *can* talk," said little Nell. "He says 'nay' as plain as possible."

"And a very *good* thing to say, my girl, when we're asked to do wrong. Don't you forget it," said her father. "But I'll tell you, wife, what made me late—I daresay you'll laugh at me a bit—but it's better to laugh than cry, and she was pretty near crying, poor body!"

"Somebody you've been helping, Jim," said his wife. "You're always giving somebody a helping hand."

"We'll, isn't that what we're in the world for? We know the meaning of mercy and loving-kindness ourselves, wife, and we've got to keep passing of them on."

"That's true, Jim," said Mrs. Barton, as she buttered the toast that Jessie had made for her father's tea; "but tell me whom have you been helping now?"

"'Twasn't much to do, but it just caught her the train," he said, between his mouthfuls of toast. "I'd put old Jack up and I was coming home, when I saw a lot of young fellows—silly chaps, old enough to know better—making fun of a queer-looking old body, the kind they calls a country bumpkin, with a great big umbrella and a big basket. She'd asked one of them the way to Paddington Station, and they was telling her all wrong and confusing of the poor old body's head. She kept dropping of her parcels, and she seemed all tired out."

"Ah! just how I felt when I first come to London; the noise do seem to turn one's head."

"Poor soul! She told me afterwards as she were servant on a farm in the country, and she's been there years and years, and she'd come up by excursion to see her married sister, that's a widow down in Deptford. And if she hadn't been and lost her purse coming back! else she'd have took a 'bus to Paddington. She'd got her return half of her excursion ticket in her glove, and she'd only twenty minutes to get the train. Well, I shouldered her baggage and cut along with her to Paddington, and saw her into the excursion, and she got me to put my name and address on an envelope she'd got in her basket, and she says she'll get her master and mistress to write and thank me, for they was dreadful anxious about her being in London alone."

"You're a nice young man, escorting of the ladies about," said his wife, laughing. "Come, Jim, drink your tea while it's hot; 'twill do you good after your cold walk."

The Bartons forgot all about the old farm-servant, but the incident was brought to mind by something that happened on Christmas Eve. On coming home with some fruit he had bought for the children, Barton found a man in the street bearing a great hamper and looking for his number.

Barton quietly unpacked the hamper at his "mate's" next door, wanting to give Bessie and the children a glad surprise; but soon he had to rush in and exhibit the turkey, and tell them of butter, and ham, and apples, and jam, and a huge cake that had come from that country farm in thankfulness for his kind act to a bewildered old body.

"Well, I never!" said Mrs. Barton; "it's quite a feast, and our neighbours must share it. Mince pies *too*, do you say? Think of that, children! That *wasn't* a day of bad luck after all, was it, Jim?"

"No, no, my girl; there's no bad luck *can* befall them as trusts the Lord and sings *thanksgiving*, whether it's sunshine overhead or clouded skies!"

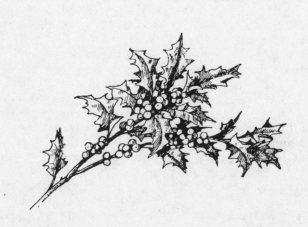

THE

WOMAN AT HOME

Annie S. Swan's Magazine

𝔓rofusely 𝔍llustrated

𝔏ondon

HODDER AND STOUGHTON

27 PATERNOSTER ROW

1895

THE CRY OF THE CURLEW.

A CHRISTMAS STORY.

By Headon Hill.

ILES upon miles of low-lying pasture land, in which, as it trended eastward, the rich grass gradually changed into sedges, the intersecting ditches broadened into dykes, the dykes in turn gaped wider and ever wider till they opened out into silent salt-fringed creeks, and the whole dreary landscape faded away—imperceptibly blended with the encroaching waters of the German Ocean. On the landward side, where the grass had as yet escaped the tidal taint, herds of cattle browsed untended; but further seaward, as the ground moistened into marshes, the only moving features in the desolate panorama were the ghost-like sails of countless windmills, which, in unceasing contest with the advancing flood, pumped the water from the sodden land.

Most of these windmills were mere skeletons, working automatically, and requiring only periodical attention. But here and there, far out toward the sea, at points where the larger dykes joined the creeks, stood windmills of more massive construction, furnished with special machinery for regulating the sluices which at intervals discharged the collected water. These more important mills were fitted with living-rooms for the men who attended to the machinery. Round these lonely habitations— often two or three miles apart, and occupied by dwellers who

endured isolation almost as complete as that of lighthouse keepers—were to be found the only signs of human life in the marshes.

It was the day before Christmas Eve. In the low-ceiled kitchen on the first floor of Wolfsdyke mill, Mark Hellyar, the keeper, sat alone. His arms were outstretched on the table before him, and his eyes stared blankly out through the opposite window across the flats. He was a big, burly man of five-and-forty, with dark overhanging brows; and, though his attitude partially suggested dejection, there was a hint in the lowering expression of his face that the dejection might very readily be exchanged for defiance. In his right hand, tightly clutched, was a crumpled letter which he had just been reading for the twentieth time that day. Even now, after a few minutes' silent rumination, he began to peruse the missive once again, using his grimy forefinger to help him spell out the words. This is what he read : —

> Knightsbridge Barracks,
> London,
> *December 22nd*, 18 —
>
> Dearest Jenny,—After many perils I am safe in England again. My first thought is of you. I am trying to get three days' furlough, and I am promised it very soon. The moment I can get away I shall hope to have a sight of your sweet face at the old spot below the mill. You remember our signal — the cry of the curlew three times repeated. When you hear that look for your true sweetheart,
>
> John Sturman.

Mark Hellyar flung the letter aside, and, rising, strode to the window, the aspect of which was neither directly landward nor directly seaward, but straight along the marshes. To the left, behind the dark line which far away in the distance marked the rising country inland, the sun was setting; while to the right and eastward a damp night mist was stealing across the lonely creeks from the sea, threatening to join forces with the twilight. Twenty yards from the windmill rolled the great dyke, which a little further down was checked by an enormous dam, half masonry and half earthwork, serving the double purpose of stemming the advancing tide, and of discharging the water from the dyke by means of a sluice.

Mark cast a searching glance over the portion of the marshes visible from the window, and, not finding what he sought, descended to the ground floor and stood in the doorway. For full a quarter of an hour he stood there motionless, peering out into the fast gathering gloom. At length with a muttered oath he returned to the room he had left, and once more seating himself at the table, began over again the task of spelling out the crumpled letter.

"She's gone to him," he

"His arms were outstretched on the table before him."

groaned, "and that's not the worst of it; she's taken away my best chance of revenge. If she had only waited I should have had them both—both at one blow. One jerk at that handle and the waters would have swallowed them up for ever," and the fierce eyes of the mill-keeper fixed their hungry gaze upon a shining lever which came through the wall and protruded into the room, the lever which controlled the sluice and set free or checked at will the swollen waters of the dyke.

"One chance is left me," Hellyar proceeded, after a pause; "he may have started before she reaches him. In that case—who knows? I may hear the signal at any moment. Ah! it's almost too big a stroke of luck to happen to the likes of me, but I'll be ready—never fear—I'll be ready for you, John Sturman, if I don't close my eyes for a year."

Taking a piece of rag and an oil can, Mark Hellyar went over to the lever and examined every bolt and joint of the connecting gear, oiling some parts and polishing others, till the whole of the machinery for liberating the pent-up waters was in thorough working order.

Then he sat down and laughed.

*   *   *   *   *

Mark Hellyar had not long been the keeper of Wolfsdyke windmill. Two years before the mill had been occupied by Jake Silvester, his wife, and his daughter Jenny. The Silvesters were not by any means a united family. Old Jake was a stern, morose man, upon whose naturally gloomy temperament the solitary life of the marshes had exercised anything but an enlivening influence. He had strict notions about parental authority, and used it unsparingly to check any symptoms of youthful exuberance on the part of his daughter Jenny, a tall, strikingly handsome girl of eighteen, with wonderful dark eyes and hair. As for Mrs. Silvester she was a nonentity, bowing in meekness to her husband's will, and living in perpetual terror of his humours.

When she was eight years old, Jenny Silvester had been sent away from the mill to live with an aunt at Lowestoft, to obtain the education which was impossible in the marshes. The girl remained in the town till she was seventeen, and it was during this period that she formed the acquaintance of John Sturman, a young man in her own rank of life, a year or two older than herself. The friendship between youth and maiden rapidly grew into a warm attachment, which increased rather than diminished in intensity when Jenny returned to her home in the marshes. Here, however, the pleasant intercourse between the young lovers received a check. Jake Silvester set his face against John Sturman, and forbade him to visit the mill. The old man had another project in view for his daughter's settlement, a project in which the principal figure was Mark Hellyar, the black-browed keeper of a mill two mills from the Wolfsdyke. Mark Hellyar was ten years older than the girl, and his uncouth manners and rough address would have been distasteful to her even if no more favoured lover had ever come to woo; but he was supposed to have saved money, and this was an unanswerable recommendation in the eyes of Jake Silvester. The keeper of the Wolfsdyke made overtures to the keeper of the Horton mill, and Mark Hellyar came over and formally "approved" of the tall girl whom he only remembered as a rough-and-tumble little lassie, given to getting periodically lost in the marshes years before. After this the two mill-keepers settled the matter in solemn conclave between themselves, and Jenny was told to consider herself betrothed to Mark.

For a time the girl held out bravely enough, and refused to listen either to her father's commands or to Mark Hellyar's clumsy pleading. Hardly a day passed but the cry of the curlew thrice repeated was heard in the neighbourhood of Wolfsdyke mill, the clandestine interviews became more frequent than ever, and it almost seemed as if the young lovers would tire the enemy out. Then, suddenly, there quickly formed one of those combinations of circumstances which without any warning sometimes swoop down on the players in a life drama, and change the entire current of the plot. First the tradesman for whom John Sturman worked failed, and after a futile search for other employment the young man, driven to his last shilling, enlisted in the Royal Horse Guards. The regiment was away fighting in Egypt, and John followed it thither as soon as his drill was learned. His departure was a sad blow to Jenny, the more especially as after his first letter from abroad no news reached her—a fact due to his appointment to the Camel Corps, at that time ubiquitous in the inaccessible regions of the Soudan. The next link in the chain was the death of Mrs. Silvester, followed, after a brief interval by the mortal sickness of old Jake himself. While the keeper of the Wolfsdyke lay dying in the turret room at the top of the mill, his daughter accorded to his weakness what she

would never have yielded to his strength. Wearied at last by the old man's querulous plaint, and convinced against her will that John Sturman's silence was only compatible with his death, Jenny Silvester listlessly promised to become Mark Hellyar's wife.

John Sturman.

A month after Jake Silvester's funeral the promise was fulfilled. A joyless wedding took place at the little village church on the edge of the marshes, and Mark led his bride straight back to Wolfsdyke mill. He had been promoted from his less important post to take his late father-in-law's place, and perhaps this was Jenny's one consolation. At least she would not have to leave the home to which she had become accustomed, and which was endeared to her by happy memories of meetings with the lover she never hoped to see again.

Mark was kind to his wife in a silent, gloomy fashion, and in time the groove of her monotonous existence ran more smoothly. By degrees she even began to have a regard for the only human being she ever saw except on her periodical shopping expeditions to the town. Husband and wife had settled down, in fact, into the ordinary humdrum life led by married folk between whom the bond is rather of respect than sympathy, when two days before Christmas a boy came along the marshes to the windmill with a letter addressed to "Miss Jenny Silvester." Mark happened to be standing in the doorway when the boy arrived. Taking the letter, he went straight to Jenny, who was busy on the floor above.

"A letter for you, my lass," he said,

abruptly. " What's yours is mine, and mine's my own. I'll open it for you."

Jenny's quick eye caught sight of her maiden name on the envelope, and the same glance recognised John Sturman's once familiar handwriting. Before Mark's slower intelligence could fathom her purpose she glided nearer to him, and with a rapid snatch possessed herself of the letter. In a moment she gained the foot of the ladder which led to the sleeping apartment above, and, quickly mounting it, disappeared through the trap-door, securing the latter behind her. In vain did Mark clamour for admission; in vain did he beat with his huge fists on the tough oaken door. The bolts were firmly shot, and Jenny sat down to read of her old sweetheart's return.

"Jenny descended into the living-room."

To Mark's surprise, after a quarter of an hour the bolt was quietly withdrawn, and Jenny descended into the living-room, very pale, but perfectly self-possessed. Her first action was to fling the letter on the table, saying :

" You can read it if you like ; it is from John Sturman. He has come back, and does not know that I am married."

Mark's face grew livid as he took the letter and spelt out the lines, every word of which was to be burned in letters of fire on his brain. When he had finished reading he tossed the paper aside as though it had stung him.

" The cry of the curlew ! " he hissed, " the cry of the curlew ! Mark you, Jenny, if that sound is heard in the marshes it will be a death knell." And without waiting for a reply he went out to prowl amongst the dykes and feed the fire of his unreasoning jealousy.

Two hours later, when he returned to the mill, Jenny was gone.

* * * * *

Slowly the twilight thickened into the darkness of night, and silently the curling wreaths of mist rolled up from the sea. By the time Mark Hellyar had done oiling the gear it was so dark that he had to light the lamp, and this simple duty changed his mood for the moment. It carried his mind back to the lonely days at the other mill, and he thought how of late his wife had relieved him of all the little household functions which he had been wont to do for himself ; thought, too, that the trivial offices had been more kindly rendered during the past few months. He had almost begun to hope that Jenny was becoming really reconciled to her lot, and that in time he might even fill the void in her heart. The thought of this maddened him again, and he fell to cursing the luck that had brought this young man back from the grave to blight the dearest wish of his life just as it seemed about to be fulfilled.

In his wrath he rose and paced the circular room. Plan after plan he formed for compassing his vengeance. He would follow his wife on the morrow and slay both of those who had wronged him ; he would brand them with infamy, and then kill himself ; he would wait at the mill in the hopes of John Sturman having started before Jenny reached him, and then——

Mark Hellyar paused suddenly in the midst of his tramp and listened. For shrill and clear through the calm stillness of the night rose the mournful shriek of the curlew, beginning as it were afar off, and quavering into the fulness of its plaint to die away, as it had commenced, with one wild note of deep despair. There was no doubt about it ; that was the curlew's cry, or rather a very good imitation of it, Mark thought, as he waited with every nerve strained for a repetition. Yes ! there it was again, the same lingering wail, and once more, for the third time, the long weeping cry thrilled the eager ears of the keeper of the Wolfsdyke.

Mark sprang forward, a cruel smile upon his face. With one mighty wrench he pulled the lever down, and lower and lower still, till it clicked in the notch, which signified that the sluice was open to its fullest capacity and that the floodgates were set free. Rushing to the window he threw it open, and then he knew at once that the machinery had not played him false. The dull rumble of the torrent as it spouted and leaped and roared from the dam told him that his work was done, and that the waters of the dykes were joining with the waters of the creeks to flood the marshland for a mile around. The tide wanted two hours of the full, and not till it had risen and ebbed again would there be a spot of dry land in the neighbourhood of the Wolfsdyke. Mark stood listening far into the night, heedless of the white fog that came drifting through the open window. It was not till towards morning, when the sounds told him that the waters were subsiding, that nature asserted herself and he fell asleep.

All the next day Mark Hellyar went about his usual avocations like a man in a dream. His rage and bitterness had died out of him with the consummation of his vengeance, and he set himself to speculate on the probable time of his wife's return. He seemed to take it for granted that now that her quest was useless she would hasten back to the mill, and things would go on as before. He did not mean to blame her for what she had done; he merely rejoiced that the cause of trouble between them was removed. Over and over again, as he pottered about the dam and refixed the sluices, he thought how lucky it was that those two had crossed on their journey, and that somewhere down there by the creeks, or perhaps washed right out to

sea, the enemy who would have injured him lay unknelled and graveless.

Night came down upon the marshes again, but still Mark was alone in the mill. His wife had not returned. He was not greatly surprised at her absence, for doubtless she would be making enquiries as to her old sweetheart's whereabouts. Mark chuckled to himself as he thought of the fruitless errand, and came to the conclusion that it didn't really matter whether she came back to-day or to-morrow or the day after. Nothing really mattered now—since the cry of the curlew had given him his vengeance.

"We had best not meet again."

Jenny was sure to return sooner or later.

On the morning of the second day, which was Christmas, Mark's work took him out across the marshes to inspect a skeleton mill that stood some way from the Wolfsdyke. His path led him landward, in the direction which people took who came out from the nearest village. Thus it was that when he had gone some distance he espied a lad coming to meet him along the edge of the dyke, and he recognised the boy as one who brought letters on the rare occasion when there was anything for the mill.

"Two for the missus in one week," said the boy, handing him a letter; "you'll be wanting a post office out here soon."

Mark Hellyar made no reply. He was staring at the envelope as though he had seen a ghost. It had been posted in London the day before—the office stamp told him that, and it was in the handwriting which had wrought such havoc in his household. But there was a difference in the mode of address. The other letter had been addressed to "Miss Jenny Silvester;" this one was plainly superscribed "Mrs. Hellyar." What could have happened? Had Jenny found John Sturman after all? If not, how could he know of her marriage? But above all, how was it that he was alive and well in London yesterday to write letters when Mark had thought that he was— Was it possible that

" He was as men are on the verge of madness."

those cries were really the cries of the curlew, attracted possibly in the mist by the lights of Wolfsdyke mill?

All this passed through his mind in a flash of time. He tore open the envelope and found a letter and an enclosure. Sitting down on the dyke-side he read Sturman's letter first. It was in these words :—

Knightsbridge Barracks,
December 24th, 18—

DEAR JENNY,—I need not say what a trouble your letter has been to me. My letters to you from the Soudan must have been lost; I wrote several. But it is no use repining now; and, as you say, now that you are married it will not do for us to meet again. I am glad to hear that you are happier than at first, and trust all will be well with you always. Goodbye, from

Your true friend,
JOHN STURMAN.

P.S.—I return your own letter to me, in case your husband should want to know what you have written about. I would not make trouble for the world.

"Shut up that noise, will you?" said Mark to the post boy who had stood idly by, whistling while the mill-keeper read. The lad moved away, to amuse himself by throwing stones into the dyke, and Mark turned to the enclosure, which he saw was in his wife's handwriting. It was dated two days before from the Wolfsdyke mill and was as follows :—

DEAR JOHN,—Your letter came to-day, and I cannot tell you that I was as glad to get it as I might have been in other days, because I was married to Mark Hellyar over a year ago. Of course you must not come here now, and, indeed, we had best not meet again. My husband treats me kindly in his way, and I am beginning to get fond of him. He was dreadfully upset about your letter to-day, and I am going to tramp into Lowestoft now to post this, so that there may be no chance of your coming here to upset him. I shall not get back till late.

Your friend,
JENNY HELLYAR.

As Mark finished reading, and while his slow intelligence was just grasping the fact that his wife was not only true to him but was also missing, the post boy stopped throwing stones into the dyke and called out—

"Master Hellyar! Master Hellyar! come quick, here's a gal's hat in the water!"

Mark ran to the spot in frantic haste, a half-formed fear struggling to take shape in his mind. It was quickly realised. Down there, caught among the sedges at the brink of the brimming dyke, floated a woman's straw hat, its poor bedizenment of artificial roses all bedraggled, and bobbing and twirling with each skurry of the salt-laden breeze. Mark knew those roses well. They told him that the victim whom his mad passion had overwhelmed on the threshold of the home she had brightened was his own true and faithful wife. One sharp pang of agony let the light into his sluggish brain at last, and he saw clearly enough what had happened. Jenny had posted her letter and was returning across the marshes ; one of those thrice-accursed fowl had chanced to cry ; his own cruel hand had done the rest.

Mark Hellyar fished the hat out of the dyke and stood smoothing out the crumpled petals of the flowers. The boy, ignorant of Mrs. Hellyar's absence, but scenting the excitement of tragedy in the mill-keeper's grim countenance, found courage to blurt out :

"A lass drowned, maybe ?"

Mark shook his head. He had not heard the words addressed to him, and the gesture meant merely that he did not want to talk ; but the boy took it as a literal negative, and went off whistling along the marshes. When he had gone a good way Mark sat down by the dyke and stared at the water. He was not thinking of its inky depths ; his mind was busy with the potentialities of what might have been. But at last the water forced itself on his attention, and he shuddered as he realised that it was his confederate. Even now he was too numbed for the luxury of grief. He was as men are on the verge of madness.

But good angels are busy in the lower world on Christmas morning, and some bright spirit, pitying the dark nature stricken low, prompted the ringers far off in the distant village to peal the joy bells early to-day. As the blessed music of the chimes was borne faint but rhythmical on the crisp air to the man by the dyke-side, it carried him back to his wedding day, and the suggestion brought the relief of tears. Mark bowed his face over the poor draggled hat and wept ; wept not only for what he had lost, but that he had lost so much more than he knew that he possessed ; wept, too, tears of repentance for the deed he had done.

And then the good angel came nearer and laid his hand on Mark's shoulder, though when he looked up wondering, all he saw was the very human form of his successor at Horton mill. Will Western was a stranger to the district and had never yet

'Jenny looked up at him and smiled."

visited the Wolfsdyke, though he and Hellyar had met frequently while about their occupation in the marshes.

And then the angel spoke, but the voice was the voice of Will Western the mill-keeper.

"Cheer up, Mark," he said ; "there ain't no call for ye to grieve, man—unless it be as you must buy the missus some new head gear. She's safe enough over at my place. Doctor says she'll be all right in a day or two."

Mark passed his hand across his eyes ; he was too dazed for speech.

"It's true what I'm telling you," proceeded Western. "I fished her out of the flood a

ile down yonder two nights agone, nigh
rowned. She's been light-headed, and only
aid who she was when she come to this
norning, or I should have been over to you
efore. Whatever ailed the sluice to go and
ip like that? Some'at wrong with the gear,
'm thinking."

Mark disregarded the question. Technical
etails, and it might be excuses, would have
o wait.

"I must go to her, Will," he said simply,
wringing the other man's hand.

And so a little later, under his comrade's
hospitable roof, Mark Hellyar knelt at his
wife's bedside, sobbing thankfully; and as
the distant bells pealed out across the marshland their glad refrain of peace on earth and
goodwill to men, Jenny looked up at him
and smiled. The Christmas angel had come
to stay.

CHRISTMAS GIFTS MADE AT HOME.

The season of Christmas is essentially one which makes heavy demands on the purse, and that much used article is, then most of all liable to show signs of exhaustion. How, in this case, are the annual gifts for relations and friends to be contrived? There is but one answer, and that suggests itself: our Christmas gifts must be made at home. The few with unlimited means at their command may choose from the ready-made treasures on view in the shops, but the many must have recourse to their stores of scraps and pieces of various materials, and concoct with these the useful and ornamental trifles which they need.

It is for the benefit of home workers that these hints are given, and they shall be devoted to articles dainty rather than costly, simple rather than elaborate.

There is figured first a hanging case for pens and pencils. Two pieces of card are required, one for the back and a much shallower but wider

section to form the pocket in front. Both sections should be covered with grey kid and lined with satin to match, or with some pretty bright colour. The holes for the ribbon are made with a very sharp stiletto, which should bore them quite cleanly through all the three thicknesses. The ribbon should be *fraise*, or to match the lining, and the cord also is grey and coloured.

The case as here pictured measures only about nine inches long by five wide, but made larger, say about twelve inches by six and a half, it may be utilised for holding a small ball of twine, scissors, a knife, one or two labels, a red or blue chalk pencil, and similar requisites for packing small postal parcels.

Or again, it may be used merely for string and scissors, the latter to be pendant down one side from a length of the cord or of the ribbon, the ball of twine to be in the pocket in a small round silk bag. This bag is easily made from a circle of silk, the diameter of which must measure three

Fig. 1.

times that of the ball of string. The silk is hemmed all round, and a running to hold an elastic made in it a third part away from the edge. Thus, if the elastic be tight enough, is formed a little globular bag, from the top of which the end of the twine escapes, but the ball cannot be taken out or in, except by stretching the elastic. Lastly, the silk bag is tacked into the pocket, and it is no disadvantage if the heading of it peeps out over the top.

The amateur painter or embroideress can of course find scope for her energies here, either on the back or on the pocket. By making the front section of plush or brocade, no need for further decoration will be found.

The next cut shows a rather more elaborate piece of work in the shape of a little horn, which is intended to be hung from a projecting bracket near an invalid's bed, and to hold a cup of milk or water, or a vase of flowers. The foundation is of strong card rolled round like a sugar-paper, and cut to shape; the lining is made of crimson satin quilted, so is very soft; the covering is a scrap of figured silk, which has a cream - coloured background, with a crimson pattern upon it. Nothing which can worry the eyes or tempt to incessant counting must be chosen. The bows are of cream-coloured satin rib-

Fig. 2.

bon, and on the lower one may be sewn a hook for the suspension of a fan. On the upper bow a hook for a watch may be added; and there is plenty of space in the intervening loop of ribbon to push a newspaper or pocket-handkerchief. The cord should be crimson and cream in colouring, and if when the horn is full the weight of the contents throws out the balance and endangers its safety, it is easy to add a second knot of cord at the point, and to secure the holder to the wall by this also. As another hint,

Fig. 3.

it may be suggested that if the card be exceedingly firm, or the silk thin, an interlining of thin flannel should be introduced, and this must be very smoothly put in, no fold or double layer being anywhere left.

This holder may be made much smaller for a tidy or spill-cup, or larger, to contain balls of wool, waste paper, or even umbrellas. By sewing a circle of card, covered with lining on both sides, into the bottom—of course first cutting off the point—the horn can be made to stand. If this is done, the lower bow of ribbon must be considerably raised. When made on a large scale, a covering of cretonne is appropriate and effective, and a lining of coloured linen or cotton.

Fig. No. 3 is a picture-easel made from the lid of a disused box, and its simplicity is its chief merit, since it is not designed to support an elaborate artistic production, but to display for a time a favourite card or photo which can be easily changed. For an invalid's room these easels will be found very useful, as they can be made to show in a few minutes as many pictures as a scrap-book could contain.

77

The way in which an easel is made is so plainly shown in the illustration that words are hardly needed. The box-lid must be a stout one, and one rim and about an inch of two others are left; all the rest is cut neatly away. The short pieces must of course be both exactly alike in size. The box is covered inside and out with Japanese paper for temporary purposes; for more lasting use with old gold satin, tan-coloured leather, or with brocade. Of course if either of these last three fabrics be chosen, the lid will have to be taken to pieces, and afterwards, when covered, sewn together again; if paper is used for it a clever worker can easily manage neatly without dismembering it, but it is advisable to strengthen all the joins with an inch-wide strip of muslin pasted over them on both sides before the ornamentation is added. Leather paper, by the way, sticks firmest when a mixture of liquid glue and paste is used for the purpose. The cord which supports the picture has hitherto passed unnoticed. It is merely threaded through two opposite holes and a knot tied in it at both ends. If the easel is covered with any material that frays easily, the cord must be sewn on and to the inside to save making the eyelet holes.

A foot or rest of cardboard about a third as high as the back, and about an inch wide, may be glued on with a muslin hinge, to serve as a support and permit of the easel being sloped to any desired angle, this piece of card being, it is

Fig. 5.

the width. If the box is in good condition staining or enamelling is all that it will require, but if very shabby or inclined to drop to pieces it is easy to cover and line all the sections with cretonne or thin tapestry, interlined with flannel if the sharp corners show signs of poking through.

Next is shown a post-card case, which also can be made from a cardboard box. If the box just holds a packet of cards comfortably, so much the better; if it is too large it must be cut to size, or failing this, made up entirely by the worker from a piece of cardboard. Supposing that a small candle-box has been found to be appropriate, take away all four rims from the lid and take the bottom of it to pieces also. Cut a triangular-shaped piece out of the bottom, as shewn in the illustration, and keep three of the four rims. There are now five pieces of card; cut a duplicate of each in brown paper and cover the papers with pink satin. Cover the cards with brown bengaline on which, for the front of the case, you have embroidered the word " Post-cards," and a flourish under it. Sew all the pink portions each to its corresponding brown cover, then sew these doubled sections together in their proper box-like form, finally attach a loop of gold cord to the back of the case, and to one side of it an indelible pencil lashed on to a length of cord.

At the back, about half an inch from the top, a paper fastener is pushed in from the outside and opened out loosely inside. Then about two dozen pieces of paper all the same size (that is,

Fig. 4.

needless to say, covered to accord with the rest of the case. Then again, by adding a ring at the top, or by sewing on a loop of cord, our easel can be made to hang.

From a wooden box a book-rest can be made on this principle, the chief difference being that the back must be greatly lower in proportion to

78

an inch smaller each way than the back of the box), are threaded together on a fine cord and attached by a loop of this round the paper stud. These papers will often be found useful for making lists, memoranda, etc., upon. Failing them a piece of card bearing a table of postal rates or similar information may be substituted.

To make a pen-wiper (No. 5) of this shape, cut a long strip of black cloth, fine felt, or cashmere, about five inches wide, pink out the lower edge of it and pleat it up into a bell-like shape. It is better to do this than either to gather the upper edge or to roll up the strip, as these last ways of

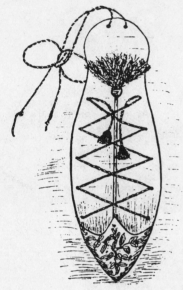

Fg. 6.

going to work make the little bundle too firm and even. When deemed the right shape, gather up closely along the upper edge with a strong thread, and add a second running about an inch lower down. Take next a strip of grey felt four inches wide, and long enough to wrap loosely once round the cashmere roll. Seam the two short edges together, run a draw-thread along the upper edge of the hoop just made, and slip it on over the black inside part, drawing it in very tightly round the lower row of gathers on the cashmere. That it may set closely, somewhat like the skirt of a doll over its petticoats tack down the lower edge of the grey here and there to the black pinking. Lastly, take a strip

of dark blue silk of thin texture and also about four inches wide. Seam this also up, and cut the lower edge of it into eight or nine scallops of alternating depths, all bordered with fine gilt gimp and lined with blue fringe, gore this sort of over-skirt slightly at the two sides and pucker it in slightly over the grey felt, running in for this purpose a draw-thread about an inch below the upper edge of the silk which now stands out round the top of the roll of cashmere. Cover this black part with the silk by turning in the latter material and pushing all folds towards the inside ; put in also snippings of flannel, cotton-wool, or anything soft, as if you were stuffing a cushion. Sew up and make neat at the top, working in a large brass curtain ring to serve as a handle ; lastly pull and knead the top with the fingers to make it a good ball-shape and firm. The monogram was not mentioned before, as it was not deemed a necessary adjunct. It should, of course, be worked on the silk before the pen-wiper is made up, and the easiest way of doing this is by tacking down fine gold thread, the ends of which are passed with a bodkin or large-eyed needle through to the wrong side of the work, and there sewn down. The silk under the monogram should be lined, to give a little extra firmness.

Lastly, we give a slipper-shaped holder for a feather broom. The foundation of the sole is of cardboard ; two similar pieces are needed, each covered with Tussah silk and sewn together all round. The pocket, or toe portion, is cut from buckram, and is a trifle wider than is the sole ; it should be covered with a piece of wash-leather richly embroidered in shades ranging from pale dull yellow to bright brown, and is brightened up with gold thread. The cord is of yellow (or tinsel) and brown silk, and does not really pass through the sole, but is sewn down to it and the stitching concealed by small flat bronze buttons. The lacing across the sole by which the broom is kept in place is similarly managed ; ten buttons being sewn on (five on each side and at regular intervals) to the front card before the two sole pieces are joined together ; the cord is then secured with the buttons, being only left free at the top where it can be knotted or tied. The tension of it must be carefully managed, as if put on too loosely it will sag, while if over tight there will be no room for the broom behind it. To those who have never tried the work we can say that embroidering upon this soft leather is by no means the unpleasant task which they might suppose it to be ; the needle chosen should be fine, and above all very sharp ; directly it becomes at all blunted and stretches instead of piercing the stuff it must be thrown aside.

COOKERY.

A CHRISTMAS DINNER.
Hare Soup.
Boiled Turbot.
Roast Beef. Boiled Turkey.
Mashed Potatoes. Broccoli.
Plum Pudding. Mince Pies.
Raspberry Trifle.
Biscuits. Cheese. Celery.
Grapes. Bananas. Walnuts.
Dessert Biscuits.
French Sweets. Chocolate.

If some of our readers think we are giving a menu far beyond what a small income can afford, to such we say, " Christmas comes but once a year, and when it comes it brings good cheer." But a very good dinner can be got by omitting some of the items. For instance, those who have only one servant might leave out the fish and the trifle. But it is wonderful what a few hours of patient, skilful work can accomplish.

HARE SOUP.

To make five pints of soup a fair-sized hare will be required. Cut it in small pieces, except the middle part of the back which should be kept whole. Take also one pound shin of beef, remove all fat and marrow from it ; a quarter pound of lean ham, one pound of bones, two carrots, two large onions, a slice of turnip, four inches of celery, flavourings of marjoram, thyme, and bay leaf, four cloves, ten pepper-corns and a little salt. Put the head of the hare, the beef, bones, vegetables, and all the seasonings into a saucepan containing seven pints of cold water. When this boils, skim it carefully and put in the pieces of hare. Boil for three hours. It should be skimmed three times during the first hour. The middle cut of the back should be taken from the saucepan after being cooked for an hour and a half, and it can be made into an entrée or supper dish, as the soup will be quite rich enough without it. When the soup has boiled the full time strain it, pound or mince the meat from the hare ; return it to the saucepan with the strained soup and three tablespoonfuls of flour mixed into a gill of ketchup and the same of port wine. Boil ten minutes to cook the flour thoroughly. Skim the soup once more. If the blood of the hare is added it must be done just before it is to be served, as boiling curdles the blood.

BOILED TURBOT.

After such a rich soup we recommend a simple mode of cooking fish. If turbot is too expensive, haddock, which at this season is excellent, can be substituted. Serve with the fish a good sauce made of two ounces of salt butter, two ounces of finest flour, a gill of the liquid the fish was boiled in, half a pint of milk, a tablespoonful of cream, salt and white pepper. Boil the sauce seven minutes. Garnish the edge of the dish with tufts of parsley and thin rounds of beetroot.

ROAST BEEF.

A clever housewife in arranging her Christmas dinner will not leave the choice of the roast to a servant, or be content with merely writing an order to her butcher for a roast weighing about fourteen pounds, but will go and see her roast cut. She will choose a sirloin with a thick undercut, red, juicy flesh, a good proportion of fat well mixed with the lean ; she will ascertain that it has been properly hung for a sufficiently long time. If her cook is untrained she will also see that the roasting fire is a clear one, that when it has to be made up it is replenished at the back. If the front of the fire gets low it should be filled up with cinders and not with fresh coals, which will smoke and be of no heating value for a quarter of an hour, whereas cinders will be at white heat in five minutes. The roast should be firmly tied with tape, and the hook of the jack be fixed in the tape, not in the meat. For the first quarter of an hour the meat should be as near the fire as possible, after that, and until the last quarter of an hour, place it where it will cook slowly but thoroughly. Baste it every few minutes. The best time to salt the meat is about ten minutes before it is taken off the jack. Allow from eighteen to twenty minutes for each pound of beef. Remove all the fat from the gravy, and in kindness to the carver, send the gravy in a sauce-boat to table. Horse-radish, scraped and put in tufts on the dish, is the most appropriate garnish for this most deservedly popular of all English joints.

BOILED TURKEY.

Large turkeys are not suitable for boiling, and the hen bird is preferable, as the flesh is whiter. Truss the bird in the same way as a fowl, cutting the legs from the middle joint and forcing them under the "apron," that is, the flexible part of the skin.

Wash the inside of the turkey with vinegar and water. Stuff it with a plain forcemeat of breadcrumb, pepper, salt, thyme, grated lemon rind, marrow fat or chopped suet, and bind these together with yolk of egg. To whiten the turkey rub it with the juice of a lemon or tie it in a floured cloth. Put it into salted water, nearly but not quite boiling, and for flavouring add two carrots and a small stick of celery. Cook it from an hour and three quarters to two hours, according to its size. Serve with boiled ham or tongue if possible, and garnish the dish with boiled carrots. Pour a plain white or parsley sauce over the turkey.

PLUM PUDDING.

We give a recipe for a rich plum pudding, but some of our ingredients can be kept back. However, we are sure no one who tries this Christmas pudding will grudge the little extra expense, as it will be amply repaid in goodness and lightness. One pound and two ounces of kidney suet chopped very fine ; one pound of breadcrumbs ; a quarter of a pound of Indian cornflour ; one pound of large raisins, stone them and cut each in half ; fourteen ounces of sultanas ; half a pound of French plums cut in slices ; half a pound of currants ; one pound of sugar ; six ounces of mixed peel cut in small pieces or shred, three ounces of pounded almonds, a pinch of salt, a teaspoonful of allspice, a grating of nutmeg, half a teaspoonful of cinnamon, a teaspoonful of baking powder. When all these dry ingredients are very thoroughly mixed in a large basin, bind them together with the juice of a lemon, eight or nine eggs which have been whipped seven minutes, a glass of brandy, and either a gill of sherry or of strong ale. The former is the more delicate, but the latter is the older mode of "wetting" the Yule pudding. Many prefer to use milk for this purpose. It should be of the consistency of a very moist dough. This quantity will make one very large or three small puddings. Boil the latter in buttered moulds for six hours ; the former should be put into a cloth which has been scalded and floured and boiled nine hours. Send the pudding to table with brandy burning on it and a hedge of holly round it.

The following is the sauce we recommend. Put into a saucepan the yolks of two eggs, the juice of a lemon, an ounce of pounded almonds which have been boiled for ten minutes, a glass of sherry, half a glass of brandy, four lumps of sugar, a gill of water. Whisk rapidly all the while it is on the fire, but do not let it come quite to boiling point. Keep the sauce hot in a *bain-marie*. We recommend this delicate and pretty-looking sauce for plain rice or tapioca puddings. If this sauce is thought too rich, make one of a large tablespoonful of arrowroot, half a pint of water, a glass of sherry, two ounces of sugar. Boil four minutes.

MINCE PIES.

Mincemeat must be made early in December, or it will not be fit for use at Christmas. It is often made without beef, but it is not so good if made merely of fruits and seasonings.

We give the ingredients required for three dozen small mince pies. One pound of large raisins, stone them and chop them small, a quarter of a pound of currants, one pound of sultanas, three-quarters of a pound of lean roast beef under-cooked, mince and pound it, half a pound of suet chopped as fine as to look like breadcrumb, one pound of sugar or a little more if liked sweet, four ounces of dates cut in small pieces, two large apples chopped fine, half a pound of mixed peel, which should be shredded, three ounces of pounded almonds, the juice of two lemons, a large grating of nutmeg, a pinch of ground cloves, a teaspoonful of cinnamon or allspice, a pinch of salt, a glass of brandy and two of sherry. After these ingredients have been well mixed, put them into a close fitting stone jar, press them very firmly, cover with paper dipped in whisky, and over the cover of the jar put a gummed paper, and in sixteen days the mincemeat will be ready for use

Line the patty tins with good puff paste a quarter of an inch thick. Put a large spoonful of the mincemeat into each ; cover with puff paste of the thickness before mentioned, and bake slowly for half an hour or forty minutes. The pies should be put into a brisk oven for the first ten minutes to raise the pastry, after that moderate the heat. When they are baked, brush them over with water and sprinkle castor sugar on them. Decorate the plates on which the mince pies are served with variegated holly.

Mince pies will keep good for two months if kept in a close tin.

RASPBERRY TRIFLE.

Line a flat crystal dish with sponge rusks or stale sponge cake ; cover the rusks or cake with raspberry preserve, and soak in a syrup made as follows. Into a saucepan put half a pound of raspberry jam, the juice of a lemon, half a teaspoonful of essence of vanilla, an inch of cinnamon stick, two ounces of lump sugar, a quarter of an ounce of dissolved gelatine, and half a pint of water. Boil ten minutes ; add a glass of sherry, and when nearly cold strain the syrup over the rusks. Cover the trifle with a pint of whipped cream made quite stiff. Dot small pink biscuits or dried cherries over the trifle.

TABLE DECORATION.

Now that the flower gardens are nearly desolate, we must go to the shrubbery, the woods, or the conservatory for leaves to embellish our table, and as our dinner is a Christmas one, the place of honour must be given to the holly, which with an abundance of its red berries might be put in a round or oval dish in the centre of the table. To take off the rather hard metallic look of the leaves put mistletoe along with it. Half way down the table place a plant of white camellia or azalea with maidenhair fern on both sides, and if it can be procured, a poinsettia might be placed near the top of the table, that is, if the table is a large one. At each guest's place put a small, narrow glass vase with a piece of maidenhair fern and mistletoe, or the fern and a small sprig of straw-coloured holly.

Fold the table-napkins in the mitre shape, and put a tiny piece of holly with berries on each. If the poinsettia be on the table, the embroidered table centre, if one be used, should have plenty of blue in it ; should the plants be white or pale pink azaleas, the embroidery might be of Indian red and gold.

THE CHILDREN'S CORNER.

A PARTY SUPPER DISH.

"Oranges and Lemons."

Boil ten ounces of Carolina rice, one ounce of arrowroot, the rind of a lemon cut thin, and four ounces of sugar in two and a half pints of sweet milk. Flavour it with ten drops of vanilla essence. Boil this till it is quite firm, but not mushy. When it is cooked turn it into a large flat dish, and when nearly cold mould it into balls the shape of oranges and lemons. To do this flour the hands, and it will be quite easily managed. When the oranges and lemons are shaped, dip them in a confection made as follows. We take the oranges first. One pound of lump sugar, the juice of three oranges, half an ounce of dissolved gelatine, half a pint of water. Boil ten minutes. Take half of the syrup and put a pinch of saffron in it. When the syrup is well coloured and nearly cold, brush the oranges over with one or two coats of it and lay them on a sieve to dry. Cover the lemons with yolk of egg and the juice of a lemon, and when they are dry brush them with the syrup which has no saffron in it. When the oranges and lemons are quite dry, arrange them on small branches of bay leaves, making them look as if they were growing. Serve a plain thick custard sauce and chocolate biscuits with them.

PLAIN DINNERS FOR DECEMBER.

Sunday —

Roast Ribs of Beef. Potatoes. Cabbage.
Apple Dumplings.

Monday —

Pea Soup (made from bones of yesterday's Roast).
Minced Beef from yesterday's Joint.
Mashed Potatoes.
Ground Rice Pudding.

Tuesday—

Stewed Chops with Carrots. Potatoes.
Fried Slices of Ground Rice Pudding—remains of yesterday's Pudding—with Red Currant Sauce.

Wednesday —

White Potato Soup.
Roast Pork. Apple Sauce. Baked Potatoes.

Thursday —

Rice Soup.
Cold Pork with Apple Sauce. Winter Greens
Ginger Pudding.

Friday—

Fish Pie.
Stewed Steak. Onions.
Marmalade Pudding.

Saturday—

Boiled Mutton. Mashed Turnips. Potatoes.
Fried Sandwich Pudding—from Marmalade Pudding.

Sunday—

Mutton Broth – from stock of yesterday's Boiled Mutton.
Beef Steak Pie. Fried Potatoes.
Baked Apples.

Christmas Day—

Hare Soup.
Roast Beef. Potatoes. Cauliflower.
Plum Pudding. Or our complete *Menu.*

Tuesday—

Fricassée of Hare —from yesterday's Soup.
Cold Beef. Stewed Potatoes.
Mince Pies.

Wednesday—

White Soup made from the stock the Turkey was boiled in.
Hashed Beef. Carrots.
Cheese and Biscuits.

Thursday —

Cold Turkey and Ham. Mashed Potatoes.
Jam Roly-poly with sweet White Sauce.

Friday—

Brown Soup (made of stock from bones of Christmas Roast).
Minced Turkey with Macaroni.
Stewed Apples.

Saturday —

Boiled Haddocks.
Stewed Shin of Beef with Turnips and Onions.
Toasted Cheese.

Sunday—

Fish Soup (made from fish and the liquid yesterday's fish was boiled in).
Roast Mutton. Browned Potatoes.
Plum Pudding.

IN SEASON IN DECEMBER.

Fish.—Cod, flounders, dory, oysters, mullet, smelts, haddock, eels, skate, turbot, soles, brill, halibut, whiting, prawns.

Game.—Grouse (out of season early in December). hares, snipe, partridge, pheasant, woodcock, wild duck.

Meat.—Beef, mutton, doe venison, pork.

Poultry. - Geese, turkeys, quails, chickens, capons, pigeons.

Vegetables.—Broccoli, cabbages, Scotch kale, leeks, carrots, turnips, potatoes, celery, onions, Jerusalem artichokes

Fruit.—Medlars, oranges, grapes, pears, apples, walnuts.

A CHRISTMAS GHOST STORY.

By Percy Andreae,

Author of 'Stanhope of Chester.'

 WAS miserable. What a fool I had been. Why had I come here? Why hadn't I refused this invitation like a man, and spent my Christmas in my chambers, or with my old maiden aunt in Drearington, or anywhere —anywhere but just here, where I knew I should be so unspeakably miserable?

You need not sneer and snigger, my doughty reader. You've been in love yourself, don't tell me, and if you haven't you ought to have been, and if you have you ought to know better, and, once more, if you haven't, then don't read my story, but leave it to your betters.

I shall never forget that New Year's Eve at Mount Edgmont, for the simple reason that I had never felt more miserable in my life. Mount Edgmont, as the reader probably knows, is the principal seat of the Duke of Teignmouth, and one of the oldest family estates in England. Reginald de L'Isle, the Duke of Teignmouth's only son, and I had been chums at Eton. Evelyn de L'Isle, the Duke of Teignmouth's only daughter and Reggy's younger sister—the sweetest girl that ever breathed—had in former days been—well, a sort of chum of mine too, when I used to spend part of my holidays with Reggy at Mount Edgmont. I was an orphan, by name Ralph Moreton. My family was a fairly good one, but unfortunately nothing to compare with the de L'Isles, who belonged to the very highest of the land. I had a fair position in the Civil Service, and a private income of about four hundred a year—all very pleasant to a man of ordinary aspirations, but terribly inadequate to one whose friends are heirs to dukedoms and baronies, and who has the misfortune to lose his heart to one of the richest and proudest heiresses in England.

Evelyn de L'Isle had always liked me, I knew, and perhaps—if I had ventured to push myself—this liking might have ripened later on into something deeper. But how would it have ended? I knew the Duke of Teignmouth and his family pride and preju-

"Lord Bertie Goring.

dice only too well. He was as kind-hearted a man in his way as one could ever wish to meet, but still he never let you forget that he was the grand seigneur, and that there was a certain limit beyond which no advance was possible with him. As for Lady Evelyn herself, what she would have said or done, had she known of my hopeless passion, I never ventured to consider. We had always been staunch friends, and even after my schooldays were over, and we met as full-grown mortals in London society and on other occasions, she never dropped the old cordial tone towards me. But the moment I felt whither I was drifting I exerted all my power of will and drew back—alas! to no purpose, so far as my happiness was concerned. I had told myself that I was a fool, and yet grew more miserable from day to day. I had sworn I would never set foot again in Mount Edgmont or any other possession of the Duke of Teignmouth's, and kept my oath for two years, at the risk of mortally offending my best friend, Reginald de L'Isle. I had even eschewed society, and refused invitations to houses where I knew I should meet Evelyn; in short, I had accomplished unheard of sacrifices in my heroic resolve to conquer a hopeless passion — and yet here I was at last again under her own father's roof, more miserable than ever, and worse than all, I knew I had given grave offence to Lady Evelyn herself, who had noticed my reticent manner towards her, and not knowing its cause, had naturally attributed it to coldness, unfriendliness, or heaven knows what.

To increase my martyrdom, I had now learned, nay, seen with my own eyes, that I had a rival in the field—as if that made any difference, indeed. And yet I had reasons, other than those of mere jealousy, to brood despairingly over this fatal circumstance. Lord Bertie Goring, who seemed to be generally recognised as the successful suitor for Evelyn de L'Isle's hand, was an old Etonian like Reggy and myself. He was what is commonly known among young men as "a good sort after all," a term which is admittedly an apologetic one, and implies a "notwithstanding" with a more or less long tail behind it. Thus I was well aware that Bertie Goring was an inveterate gambler, a hard drinker, and generally a fast liver in every sense of the term. To see Evelyn smile upon this man, who was confoundedly good-looking too, and to know that the match between her and him was practically as settled as such things can be without the actual ratification of the contracting parties themselves—why, goodness me, need I dilate any further on all it meant for me?

On that New Year's Eve there was a grand costume ball at Mount Edgmont. I had danced once with Evelyn, and had been

refused a second dance rather coldly and haughtily. Thereupon I had placed myself —fool as I was—in a position where I could see and watch the progress of Bertie Goring's courtship. There were about two hundred guests at the ball, thirty of whom— and I amongst the number—were staying at the castle. As the night wore on I could bear the hateful strain no longer, and taking a suitable opportunity, I slipped away from the gay throng downstairs, and betook myself to the smoking-room in the eastern tower, where I passed a quarter of an hour or so in giving expression to the sentiments recorded in the first paragraph of this story.

Solitude is wonderfully solacing to a sick heart, and this room was so remote from the bustle and gaiety I had left, that I might have fancied myself hundreds of miles away from the scene of my sufferings. Knowing that none of my fellow-guests were likely to find their way through the intricate passages and corridors to this rarely visited wing of the immense mansion, I abandoned myself unreservedly to the thoughts that were tormenting me, and sat for a long while, with my arms spread on the table and my face buried in them—in an attitude, in short, which foolish people with my complaint are wont to assume on such occasions.

After a while the stillness of the place, which was only dimly lighted by one lamp with red glass hanging from the centre of the ceiling, began to tell upon my feelings, but in a curious way. While it calmed me in one respect, it seemed to impart to me a sense of unrest which I should find it difficult to explain. It struck me of a sudden that I should be missed at the ball, and that my retirement to this secluded corner of the castle would appear strange. As this thought occurred to me, I raised my head with the intention of going back and fighting out my trouble resolutely and with a calm front. There was nothing I dreaded so much, indeed, as to see the real state of my mind exposed to other eyes.

To my consternation, however, I found when I looked up that I was no longer the only occupant of the room. I blushed as I thought of the position in which I had been discovered, but the next instant I started up with an exclamation of absolute dismay, for, incredible though it seemed, my first impression was that the person sitting on the opposite side of the table, with his eyes fixed upon me with a steady, earnest gaze, was no other than the Duke of Teignmouth himself. Yet it was impossible. I remembered having seen

e Duke downstairs in the costume of a
anish grandee, while this personage was
essed like an English cavalier of the six-
enth century. The likeness, nevertheless,
s so startling that it fairly took my breath
ay, and I stood for a considerable while
ring open-mouthed at the motionless
ure in front of me. Who could it be? And
w could he have entered the room without
observing him? That he was not one of
e more intimate guests of the evening was
rtain, else I should have known him, and
t for a stranger to the house to have found

each other out of countenance for the rest of
the night.

"That is a marvellous get-up of yours," I
ventured to remark at last, by way of opening up a conversation. My own costume was
that of a Spanish toreador. "I wonder I
never noticed you downstairs."

But in lieu of a reply, my strange companion merely inclined his head very gravely,
without, however, removing his eyes from my
face, then rose from his chair, stood for a
moment drawn up to his full height, which
was very imposing, and then, again without
turning his head away from
me, glided slowly and perfectly
noiselessly out of the room.

"My strange companion."

s way unaided through all those labyrin-
ine corridors to this lonesome spot appeared
xt to impossible.

All these reflections passed through my
nd quite slowly, and an uncanny sensa-
n followed in their wake, for, while I thus
red and reflected, my companion never
ce took his eyes off my face, but sat there,
id like a figure in wax, save for that steady,
ercing gaze I have mentioned, which
ve his countenance something life-like and
al.

At last I could stand the oppressive silence
longer. After all, we could not remain
ting opposite one another trying to stare

The effect of all this upon me was so
thrilling that I felt a shiver pass through my
body from the crown of my head to the soles
of my feet, and in my agitation I started up,
overthrowing my chair, and seized by an
irresistible impulse, rushed to the door and
out into the passage in pursuit of my strange
visitant. The passage led to a winding staircase which descended to the eastern wing of
the castle, upon which the tower was built.
At the top of this staircase I saw the strange
figure, with its head still turned towards me
as before, waiting apparently in anticipation
of my following it.

I am not of a timid disposition in ordinary

parlance, but in this instance I have no hesitation in admitting that a sensation of absolute fear crept over me, and I stood for a moment irresolute whether to advance or go back to the room I had left. But before I could make up my mind either way, the figure moved on again, descending the stairs in the same gliding, noiseless fashion in which it had passed out of the smoking-room, and, obeying the same impulse as before, I moved on likewise, now, however, rather led than pursuing.

I thought I knew the ins and outs of Mount Edgmont perfectly, having spent many a summer and winter vacation during my schooldays in exploring every nook and corner of the magnificent old castle with Reggy. But it became evident to me now that I had a guide whose knowledge of its intricacies was far superior to my own. We

the dance-music and the hum of the gue in the distance, and knew that we we approaching the scene of the festivity. W my strange companion going to mix bold with the gay throng below? For a mome it shot across my mind that the whole thi might be some practical joke perpetrated my expense by Reggy himself, who w rather addicted to this questionable speci of fun. But I was soon undeceived. O sudden my guide halted at the end of a wi corridor, and, as if his movements and mi were in some way interdependent, I, to came to an abrupt standstill.

Where we were I knew not, for I ha entirely lost my sense of locality, but I cou see that six or seven paces ahead of m where the figure remained stationary, the was a door which stood slightly ajar, letti a flood of light into the passage. As I stoo and gazed, th somewhat gri features of t figure, which could plain distinguish the light fro the half-ope door, relaxed in a kindly smil as if inviting m to advance Hesitating longer, I rushe forward precip tately, but to late — before reached the spo the figure ha vanished. Wit out considerin what I was doin I pushed ope the door throug which I felt cer tain it ha passed, an burst into th room, deter mined at an cost to follo

"Fastening a fresh rose in her hair."

passed swiftly through a maze of doors and rooms and corridors, for the most part dark or very sparely lighted, now turning abruptly into some passage which apparently led to nowhere in particular, now mounting or descending staircases the locality of which I was already far too bewildered to remember. Presently I could distinguish the strains of

and gain speech of my strange acquaint ance. But the sight that met my view her made me start back in confusion. The room, fairly sized and luxuriously furnished was lighted up by a profusion of taper candles. At the further end was a hug mirror, reaching almost to the ceiling, an in front of it, tranquilly engaged in fasten

g a fresh rose in her hair, stood Evelyn de
'Isle.

She turned round with a little start as I
ntered.

"Mr. Moreton!" she exclaimed, in a tone
f surprise.

"I—I beg your pardon," I stammered,
reatly embarrassed, "I thought—I mean, I
llowed—surely he entered here."

And I looked round the room dumb-
ounded. There was no trace of any one else
ere.

"He? Who?" she asked, following my
stonished glance.

I felt dreadfully foolish. What was I to
y? I had
mmitted an
n pardonable
each of good
nners. This
as Lady
velyn's bou-
ir, as I now
cognised,
d I had burst
upon her in
is rude and
ceremonious
hion, like
me crazed
ing. There
s nothing
it but to
nfess my
lly, and
ke such ex-
ses for my-
f as I could.

"Lady Evelyn," I said, "I hardly know
w to explain; but—but I believe I have
en a ghost."

She turned pale.

"A ghost?" she said, tremulously. "What
s it like?"

I told her of my adventure, to which she
tened at first gravely. But as I proceeded
e turned her head away, and toyed ner-
usly with the lace of her dress. It struck
e that she looked confused, and a chance
ance at the reflection of her face in the
irror showed me that it was covered with
ushes. I cannot describe the sensation
e discovery produced in me. Had I been
oled after all, and did she know it? I
arcely dared to pursue the thought, and
ter I had finished my story I waited in
ence for her to speak.

The pause that ensued was painfully em-
arrassing to me, but presently she turned

her face, and looked at me with a curiously
arch expression.

"You say you went alone to the smoking-
room in the tower?" she asked.

"Yes," I answered.

"And stayed there quite alone for nearly
half an hour?"

Again I answered affirmatively.

"Why?" she asked, with a brevity which
disconcerted me not a little.

"I hardly know," I replied, trying to look
innocent. "I felt a little out of sorts, and
went there to have a few minutes' quiet."

The answer seemed to satisfy her, and she
remained silent for a moment.

"Claimed her as his partner."

"Lady Evelyn," I said, "if I have been
made the subject of a practical joke, I would
take it as a favour if you would tell me so."

"A practical joke?" she said reflectively.
"No, I think not." Then breaking off with
a little embarrassed laugh, she asked: "You
are quite sure the figure you saw smiled at
you?"

"Distinctly," I answered; and thinking it
best to treat the matter lightly, I added:
"On the whole I must acknowledge that the
ghost, if it was one, behaved most amiably."

"It does not always do so," she said. "But
I am glad it was pleasant—for your sake,"
she added, as if with an afterthought, and
again I saw a deep blush tinge her cheeks,
which made me feel uncomfortably suspicious
of having been tricked.

"Perhaps as you are here, Mr. Moreton,"
she continued, before I could speak, "you
won't mind taking me down to the ball-room,

unless you wish to resume your solitary musings in the smoking-room."

There was something so provokingly roguish in these words, and yet her manner in expressing them was so embarrassed and timid, that I felt at a loss for an answer. I gave her my arm, and we made our way in silence through the corridor which I had traversed only a few moments before, and which I now saw led to the picture-gallery adjoining the grand staircase. There were a few couples roaming about the gallery as we crossed

so, however, she remarked, drawing forth her dancing-card:

"Let me see, our next dance is the second after this, I think, Mr. Moreton. You will find me near the fountain in the conservatory."

Saying which, she deliberately drew her pencil through the name standing against the dance in question on her card, and left me standing in a transport of surprise and pleasure.

How long I remained in that attitude I can't say, but I was aroused presently by a well-known voice at my elbow, saying:

"I hastened to the conservatory."

it, and at the opposite side I recognised Bertie Goring wandering from niche to niche with a disconsolate air.

Lady Evelyn saw him too, and, stopping suddenly, turned back as if to pass out of the gallery by another door. It was evident that she wished to elude him—a circumstance that made my heart leap with a wicked joy. But the manœuvre came too late, and in another moment he overtook us, and claimed her as his partner.

I bowed silently, and Lady Evelyn transferred her arm from me to him. As she did

"Well, Moreton, you look quite awe-struck. What has happened?"

It was the Duke himself, Evelyn's father. Recollecting myself instantly, I put on a laughing face, and replied:

"You will hardly believe it, sir, but I've just seen a ghost."

The effect of my words was an unexpected one.

"What do you mean, Moreton?" his Grace said, almost sternly. "I trust you are joking."

"If it is a joke, sir," I answered, rather

ettled by his curt tone, " it is certainly not
of my making."

And I related my adventure, discreetly
omitting, however, to mention the fact of its
having terminated with my intrusion into
Lady Evelyn's boudoir.

The Duke listened with a frown that grew
deeper as I proceeded. When I had finished,
he looked at me for a moment keenly ; then,
turning sharply on his heel, he said :

" Have the goodness to follow me, Mr.
Moreton."

I obeyed silently, and he led me round the
great gallery, stopping at last before a huge
painting set in an ancient framing,
which did not hang on the wall
like the others, but was let into the
stonework like a
frieze. Pointing
to it, he said :

" Was the per-
son you saw any-
thing like that ? "

" The very
man, by Jove," I
exclaimed, for-
getting all for-
mality in my sur-
prise at the like-
ness, which was
indeed striking.

I saw the Duke
start slightly, and
give me a look
of displeasure.

" I beg, then,"
he said coldly,
" that you will
forget what you
have seen, Mr.
Moreton, and
above all that
you will not speak about it to any one,
whether it be a member of my family or not.
It is not agreeable to me that my guests
should meet with adventures of this description under my roof."

With these words he left me, considerably
perplexed. This was turning the tables with
a vengeance, I thought. After all, it was not
I who had sought the ghost's acquaintance, it
was the ghost who had sought mine, and why
this fact should call his Grace's wrath down
upon my head, I was at a loss to conceive.

I consoled myself, however, with the
thought of Lady Evelyn and her spontaneous
concession of the dance she had refused me
at the commencement of the evening, and
soon forgot all about this little incident.

As soon as the appointed time arrived I
hastened to the conservatory, where I found
Lady Evelyn already awaiting me. She rose
as I approached, and placing her arm in mine,
suggested that we should sit out the dance.
There was a shyness in her manner, so unlike
her, and yet a certain assurance withal that
made my very heartstrings quiver. I remembered having had a similar sensation two years
before, when I was first seized with my mad
infatuation, and withdrew to save myself from
the misery of a passion which I felt to be
hopeless. Ah, how ill-bred and churlish
she must have thought me ! And yet here

" I must ask you to resign Lady Evelyn to me."

I was again at her side, as madly in love as
ever.

" Mr. Moreton," she said, as we moved
on, " I wanted to ask you not to tell any one
about—about what happened to you an hour
ago. If you don't mind, I should prefer that
it remained between you and me."

" But I have already told his Grace, Lady
Evelyn," I said, with some dismay. " Had I
only known——"

" My father ? " she exclaimed. " How
very unfortunate. And did he—did he seem
surprised ? "

" I think he was annoyed, Lady Evelyn.
My adventure appeared to displease him
greatly, though it must be admitted that it
was not of my seeking."

"Perhaps he thinks differently," she answered.

Her tone seemed to imply that she herself was inclined to think differently, which only tended to increase my surprise. But before I could ask her for an explanation, our short *tête-à-tête* was brought to a premature end by the sudden appearance of the Duke himself. He approached us hurriedly from a side-

meaning of it all? What had I done to incur the anger of one who, ever since I was a boy, had always treated me with almost fatherly kindness, and had liked me too, for Reggy had often told me so?

I began to feel myself the victim of some extraordinary mystery. But if this unpleasant incident caused me trouble, what now followed affected me far more deeply.

"I can't tell you how sorry I am.'

entrance, and addressing his daughter, told her somewhat peremptorily that she was wanted in the ball-room.

"I am sorry I must ask you to resign Lady Evelyn to me, Mr. Moreton," he said, turning to me with the same look of haughty displeasure which his face had worn when he parted from me in the picture-gallery. "Some of our guests are leaving, and my daughter has to perform her duties as hostess."

And without waiting for me to reply, he gave his arm to Lady Evelyn, and led her away. I stood utterly perplexed, the more so as I thought I noticed an abashed look on Lady Evelyn's face, as she left the conservatory on her father's arm. What was the

I saw no more of Lady Evelyn that night. But the next day, and the day after, I could not but feel that my presence at Mount Edgmont had become distasteful to its proprietor. His manner towards me was as cold and distant as was compatible with the politeness of a host, and, what annoyed and puzzled me more than anything else, he seemed to be incessantly on the watch to prevent any meeting between me and Lady Evelyn. To increase my sense of discomfort, my old friend and school-fellow Reggy, who was usually heartiness itself towards me, grew of a sudden constrained and embarrassed, like one who has something weighing upon him and cannot sum up courage to come out with it.

Such a state of affairs was unendurable to me for any length of time, and at last I made up my mind to leave Mount Edgmont. When I told Reggy that I found myself obliged to return to town on the following day, a look of relief came into his face. Then he suddenly placed his hand on my shoulder, and said :

"Ralph, old fellow, why did you never tell me about this ? "

"About what ? " I asked, surprised at his sudden burst of feeling.

"I mean, about this unfortunate attachment."

"Attachment ? What are you talking about ? "

Reggy looked at me with a quiet smile.

"Ralph, my boy," he said, " I can't tell you how sorry I am. If she were in my giving, you should have her, that's all I can say. But you know the governor's strong notions on the subject."

If he had struck me a sudden blow with his clenched hand, I could not have staggered me more than his words did.

"How do you know——" I stammered.

"The governor told me himself," he said.

"The Duke ? " I exclaimed. "Impossible. Why, not even Evelyn herself dreams——"

The look of comic compassion with which he received my words made me redden with shame. I saw it all instantly. My secret had been betrayed, was perhaps the common property of the guests assembled at Mount Edgmont. By what means it had become so, I knew not, nor dared consider. But the idea itself was maddening, above all on account of Evelyn herself, for—great powers—what a confounded fool she must think me. I could not trust myself to say any more to Reggy, and left him in a frame of mind which I will leave the reader to imagine.

How I passed the remainder of that day I don't remember. I only know that I sought an interview with the Duke, and informed him of my intention to depart on the morrow. Nothing else passed between us, but his manner was unusually kind, and I think he felt sorry for me. Lady Evelyn did not appear downstairs at all that day. She was indisposed, it was said, but my own belief was that she preferred not to meet me again. To add to my mortification, I learned that Lord Bertie Goring had been closeted with the Duke for nearly an hour that morning, and had presumably made his formal proposal for the hand of Lady Evelyn.

At last the night came, and I was able to escape from the company which had become a veritable torment to me. Ah, what a night it proved ! The room I occupied was situated in the left wing of the castle, which was of comparatively modern build. Although I had retired to rest early, it was some time past midnight before I fell into a troubled sleep. There was one dream in particular which haunted me, recurring again and again with incessant repetition. I was trying to escape

" With a loud cry I sprang out of bed."

from Mount Edgmont by night, and could not. The figure I had seen in the room in the tower a few evenings ago was always at my side, and led me astray in the corridors of the castle, leaving me at last standing at the door of Lady Evelyn's boudoir, where I entered to find her, as I had found her that evening, fastening a fresh rose in her hair before the mirror. Then the vision vanished, and the dream and the unsuccessful flight began afresh, until at last I shrieked aloud in my anguish, and awoke.

For an instant I still imagined I was dreaming, for there, not three paces from my bed, standing in the moonlight which shone through the window-casement into the room, I saw that strange figure once more, its eyes now fixed upon me with a stern, angry look.

As I started up, it raised both arms aloft, and shook them menacingly. With a loud cry I sprang out of bed, and rushed at the spectre ; but before I reached the spot, it was gone.

At that moment I heard a succession of cries, which seemed to come from someone beneath my window, and almost simultaneously there was a sharp rapping at my door, and I heard a voice outside call to me to open.

Utterly bewildered, I unlocked the door,

I rushed to the casement, flung it open and looked out. The next moment I fell back laughing.

In the snow, just underneath my window, hammering with all his might against the door which led from this wing of the castle on to the terrace, stood Lord Bertie. He was —I blush to say it—in his night-shirt. How he had got there, heaven knew. But I did not stop to think or explain. Seizing the lighted candle which the Duke held in his hand, I hurried out of the room, followed by his Grace himself, and passing quickly through the corridor and down the staircase,

"I presented myself in the Duke's study."

only to start back again with an exclamation of astonishment. The person who now entered hurriedly, and with signs of extreme agitation on his face, was no other than the Duke of Teignmouth himself.

"Where is Lord Bertie ? " he asked. " His room is empty. Great God, if it should be true——"

"Goring ? " I exclaimed. " What has happened to him ? "

"I fear he has met with foul play, Moreton," the old Duke said with a white face. "I am not usually affected by dreams—but this one was fearful. I saw—hark, what is that ? " he broke off, as the cries beneath my window sounded again louder than before.

unbolted the door, and let the unfortunate fellow in.

At sight of the Duke he looked somewhat confused, but his pale face showed that he was suffering more from fright than embarrassment.

"How the deuce did you get out there Goring ? " I cried. " You must have climbed out of window. This door here was locked and bolted."

It was some time before he could find speech to explain.

"I've had the most extraordinary experience," he stuttered at last—" woke up about half an hour ago almost strangled by some masquerading fellow who had got into my room somehow. When I tried to seize him, he was out of the door like a shot, and I after him. He led me a regular dance, upstairs and downstairs, till at last he disappeared out of this door, and I, like a fool, followed. When I got outside, he was no more to be seen, and when I wanted to get back again, I found the door wouldn't open," he added viciously.

The Duke listened in silence, but his face was very grave, and he glanced at me with a curious look of interest, which emboldened me to relate my own second adventure with the ghost that night. He said nothing, save to request Goring and myself to keep the matter quiet. But when we had lighted Goring, all shivering and quaking with cold, to his room, the Duke stopped for a moment at my door, and said :

"I should like to see you to-morrow again for a few minutes, before you go, Ralph. Good night."

And with these words he left me. "Ralph, Ralph," I kept repeating to myself, as I pondered over his speech. The old Duke had not called me by my Christian name since I was at school at Eton.

The next morning at ten o'clock I presented myself in the Duke's study with a heavy heart. On my way there I had passed the conservatory, where I had seen Lady Evelyn walking with Bertie Goring, who, by the way, was afflicted with an awful cold, and by her embarrassed air and his animated manner I had little difficulty in guessing the nature of their interview.

"Sit down, Moreton," said his Grace, when I entered. "There are one or two things I wish to say to you. In the first place, I thought it might interest you to know that Lord Bertie Goring is at this moment offering his hand to Lady Evelyn."

I bowed silently. I was only too well aware of the fact.

"It is Goring's own wish to have his answer direct from her," he continued. "You probably know what it will be, Moreton."

"Your Grace," I stammered, half ashamed and half angry at what I thought a cruel and unbecoming jest.

"Well, well," he said, "Evelyn has told me that her affections have been engaged elsewhere since several years, and though I may frankly tell you that under ordinary con-

ditions I could never have consented to such a match—not that I have any objection to your personal character, my dear boy——"

I started up electrified, nearly knocking down my chair in my amazement.

"There are certain circumstances," the Duke went on, " which I dare not ignore, and which lead me to believe that you will make Evelyn a good husband. Stay," he continued, in a lower voice, seeing my movement of delirious joy, "there is one other matter

" Stood blushing and confused."

which I wish to tell you about, and which may perhaps explain a good deal that has seemed incomprehensible to you. Three hundred years ago, Moreton, an ancestor of mine, gave his only daughter away in marriage to a rich but profligate and brutal nobleman. Her husband ill-treated her, and she died broken-hearted, for she had loved a better man. Her father challenged his own son-in-law to mortal combat, and killed him, after which he shut himself up in this very castle Mount Edgmont, and died two years later, overwhelmed with shame and remorse. This is a matter of common historical knowledge. What is less commonly known is that ever since that time no aspirant to the hand of a daughter of the de L'Isles has escaped a visitation from the spectre of that most unhappy of fathers, who signifies his approval or disapproval of the intended alliance in an unmistakable manner; and woe to him who disregards it. The figure you saw and followed on that night of the ball was the ghost of my unfortunate ancestor. Had you frankly told me the end of your adventure, which I only learned yesterday from Evelyn's lips, you might have been spared the mortification you have undergone."

He rose as he spoke the last words, and laid his hand kindly upon my shoulder. Then he touched a bell on his table, and ordered the servant who entered to tell Lady Evelyn that he wished to have a few moments' conversation with her.

What I said and did I haven't the slightest recollection. I only know that when Lady Evelyn entered her father's study a few minutes later, she found me there alone, and stood blushing and confused on the threshold.

What thereupon took place, however, I remember with a distinctness that will never fade, but I fear it would scarcely sound new to any one, except perhaps the doughty reader whom I apostrophised at the commencement of my story, and him, or her, as the case may be, it would presumably no interest at all.

Besides, one must draw the line somewhere, even in a ghost story. Considering that I had never made love to Lady Evelyn it may seem strange to say that not thirty seconds after she entered the room all trace of embarrassment had vanished both from her face and mine. But then—what else but a strange sequel could be expected to so strange a wooing?

COOKERY.

MENU FOR A CHRISTMAS DINNER.

Menu.

Mock Turtle Soup.
Sole à la Colbert.
Roast Pheasants.
Boiled Turkey. Celery Sauce.
Brussels Sprouts with Cream.
Sirloin of Beef.
Braised Ham.
Christmas Pudding.
Mince Pies.
Flame Pudding.
Apples à la Portugaise.

MOCK TURTLE SOUP.

Bone half a calf's head, blanch it and cook it for two or three hours in water with salt in it. Take out the head and press it till cold. Cut into small pieces 1 lb. of veal, 2 lbs. of gravy beef, 6 ozs. of lean bacon, 1 onion, 1 carrot, 1 turnip, a celery stalk, put all these ingredients into a saucepan, and fry them a light brown in 2 oz. of butter, then add 4 ozs. of flour and brown that also, and pour in gradually 3 qts. of good stock and also the 2 qts. of liquor in which the head was boiled. Put in a bouquet garni, some peppercorns, and salt, bring the soup to the boil, skim it well, and simmer slowly for three hours. At the end of that time strain the soup and return it to the saucepan. Add a little lemon juice and the calf's head cut into neat squares, more seasoning if required, and serve very hot. Cost—7s. 6d.

SOLE A LA COLBERT.

Fillet the soles after skinning, and fold each fillet round. Butter a baking-dish, put on the fillets, sprinkle over salt and a few drops of lemon juice, cover with a buttered paper, and bake for ten minutes. When cooked put some Maitre d'Hotel butter in each fillet, and roll them in brown bread crumbs. Dish the fillets in the centre, and pour anchovy sauce round. Cost—4s.

ROAST PHEASANTS.

Draw and truss two pheasants for roasting. Cover the breasts with a thin layer of larding bacon, and roast the birds for thirty to forty minutes. Remove the bacon when the pheasants are nearly done and let them brown, then dish up and serve with gravy bread sauce and fried bread crumbs. Garnish the dish with watercress. Cost —7s. 6d.

BOILED TURKEY. CELERY SAUCE.

Truss a turkey for boiling, and put it into a large saucepan with enough second stock or boiling water to cover it, add a carrot, an onion stuck with cloves, some celery, a bouquet garni, a few peppercorns and some salt, and let it simmer very gently, skimming well, for about two hours. Drain carefully when done, dish up and pour celery sauce over it, garnish the dish with rolls of bacon and balls of veal stuffing. Cost—9s.

BRUSSELS SPROUTS WITH CREAM.

Blanch two pounds of sprouts after picking them, and let them remain in the water till very nearly cooked. Drain them and put them into a sauté pan with two tablespoonfuls of good white sauce, season them with salt and pepper and a little nutmeg, and add about a gill of cream. Heat the sprouts in the sauce, but do not let it boil, shake them lightly for ten minutes or so, then serve on a hot dish. Cost—1s.

BRAISED HAM.

Soak a ham in cold water for a day, or longer if very dry and salt. Wrap it in a thin cloth, cover with water, and simmer till barely cooked. Drain and take off the cloth, place the ham in another stewpan with some stock and prepared vegetables, and let it cook again very gently for another hour. Take out the ham, reduce the stock to a glaze, and brush the ham over with it. Place on a hot dish, and garnish with freshly-boiled vegetables cut into fancy shapes. Send brown sauce to table with it which has had two tablespoonfuls of red currant jelly put to it. Cost—14s.

FLAME PUDDING.

Cream four ounces of butter with four ounces of castor sugar till white and frothy, beat in five yolks of eggs and two ounces of blanched and pounded almonds and four ounces of sifted fine flour. Whisk the whites of the eggs to a stiff froth, stir them in lightly and make the mixture rather thick with stale cake crumbs. Butter a pudding basin, turn in the batter, and steam for an hour and a half. When done turn out the pudding and set light to it as Christmas pudding is sometimes served. Cost—1s. 2d.

APPLES A LA PORTUGAISE.

Peel and core some good white cooking apples and cook them in syrup till tender, but not out of shape. Place the apples in a deep dish, fill the centres with some red currant jelly, and decorate with glacé cherries. Boil the syrup till thick, add some of the jelly to it, and colour with cochineal to a pretty pink, then pour it round the apples. Cost—1s.

COST OF THE DINNER.

				£	s.	d.
Soup	...	..	...	0	7	6
Fish	...	...	...	0	4	0
Game	...	...	.	0	16	6
Meat	...	...	...	1	3	0
Vegetables	...	...	...	0	1	0
Sweets	...	...	...	0	7	2

		£2	19	2

Life and Work at Home.

OVER THE TEACUPS.

By Annie S. Swan.

IT has come upon me with something of a shock to realise that the year is near its close. It seems so short a span since I last through these pages wished my many friends, known and unknown, a Christmas greeting. But our slow wonder, our regrets, our fervent wishes, cannot retard the steady feet of Time. He marches on, whatever care or strife or trouble may fret the minds of men, however closely we may seek to cling to joys which much pass; he pays heed to none. And in it all is the solemn lesson read to us month by month and year by year, that the day is far spent, and soon the night of earthly life will come.

As we grow older, the years which to impatient youth seemed tardy always, speed all too quickly for us who have so much to do. This consciousness of the rapid flight of time is always the warning to us that our first youth is past. How well do we yet remember the long school terms which seemed so interminable between holiday seasons; the days which dragged so slowly from Monday morning till Friday night, when for a brief space, that halcyon Saturday, school tasks knew us no more. Alas! now we could pray the cycle to stand still, the days to tarry with us yet a little; we wish our Saturdays did not so quickly come, leaving behind a week laden with too many unfinished tasks. Even so will it be till we are called hence, leaving regretfully our life-work undone.

I write this upon a Monday morning, and to many Monday is a weary day. To those who find Sunday no day of rest, it brings a sense of reaction which is painful; to others who take up the week's burden after a brief spell of precious Sabbath rest, it seems the first long round of an interminable task. What should we do, I wonder, without the Sabbath rest? I am more than ever grateful that I have been given grace to resist all encroachments, social or otherwise, upon that day. Without its calm quiet, its absence of hurry and fever and fret, its blessed stillness unbroken by the clang of door and surgery bells I feel sure I should soon break down. Please God I shall always keep unbroken my seventh day of rest.

When one begins to see middle age looming in the distance, I suppose one's ideas change; one looks at life from a different standpoint.

96

not old as years go, but I suppose life may measured by its fulness; mine has been and full indeed. Looking back, as one of necessity ust at this season of the year, it seems so owded that even memory is at times a little rained.

There are some who never know the meaning leisure, who toil from dawn to dark, day in d day out, all the year through. These are t necessarily tillers of the soil, and much of eir work is done within the four walls of a om haunted by phantoms of lost opportunities, arren efforts, ideals unachieved. But if amid all there be the consciousness of earnest ideavour to give of the best, there is nothing st. For we cannot and will not be held sponsible for feeble work done when out of ealth and weary beyond measure; work for hich man may judge us hardly, saying, "He played out, his best work is done." Words so asily uttered, falling glibly from lips that have ever earned the right to criticise, and sinking to the sensitive heart of the tired worker like rrows dipped in gall. Well might we say, It better to fall into the hands of the living God an be left to the tender mercies of men.

These thoughts, called forth naturally at this trospective season of the year, are not put in ords through any sense of bitterness or sore-ess against those to whom my written words ave gone forth from time to time. I have but ttle reason to complain, since to me is given, an age which finds many still struggling un-knowledged, an audience which listens atten-vely and in the main most kindly to what I ave to say. Only I would here emphasise a ct I have often touched upon in these columns hen replying to individual correspondents, at the path of literature is not one of roses, and at a reputation, hardly won always, is twice as ard to sustain, and a constant source of anxiety d travail to all who pursue it.

* * *

I have letters beside me, but I think I shall ere make good a threat uttered some months go, and take all the space allotted to me for ne big talk, excusable perhaps once a ear, and at Christmas time, when nobody harshly disposed to criticism. There are ertain thoughts present in every mind this season, certain memories blossoming ith keen fragrance in every heart, certain opes for whose fulfilment, among the faith-l and believing, prayer is made. Christmas rings to us always, I think, a wafted fragrance om the suntime of our youth. As we sit dream-g now, we are surrounded by the shadows many a Christmas Day gone by; and seeing memory many loved ones on whose faces shone e Christmas joy, we marvel, being left so far hind, that Christmas joy is still possible to s. It is one of the exquisite provisions of our ature, I think, that compensations are so many d so satisfying; we lose here, and gain there; e sweet face is removed, another takes its ace, in so far that it makes the blank less

bitter; and so the gaps as we go are filled up gradually, and memory, tender always, walks with us, keeping green in our hearts all the best in what we lost, else were the world too dreary, and we fainting by the way. I would withdraw the word lost, I think, because those we have given back to God, and who visit us so vividly in memory at Christmas time, cannot be lost, only in keeping for us.

What a wonderful day that will be when we shall see face to face, when the garment of earthly vision shall be exchanged for the clear outlook of Heaven—what revelations, what boundless surprises shall await us. It will seem to us that everything is reversed. What we thought great here will be little yonder, and the weak things of this world which we have passed by will be exalted, and we shall behold them in their true light as the great things of God. Sometimes, dwelling upon this fascinating theme, one is a little impatient, longing for that clearer vision. For amid the clamour of many voices, it is so hard to know which has the true music in its ring, counterfeits are so fair; and so many name the name of Christ, not knowing Him in their hearts. In these days it becomes more and more incumbent upon the servants of God to walk warily, and to give forth no uncer-tain sound; proclaiming by deeds rather than by words upon what side they have elected to fight. Let us then, having looked back, and while humbled by the sight of our many shortcomings, ever go forward joyously, and full of hope. We have left a year behind us, but another stretches before. Achievement is still possible; there is room for our souls to live, opportunity will not lack for the exercise of our goodliest gifts. Let us anew resolve to crush in us what is mean and sordid and abasing, and cultivate that part of us which is divine. Constant aspiring, even when accompanied by many failures, is bound to work its perfect work in us. It is glorious to look up. The sky is above us. Let us lift our eyes to it, and find there the purity, the strength, the consolation we need when we wish to fight the unseen foes which visit every human heart.

* * *

To me personally, the year has been full of eventfulness, and much joy has lightened labour. It opened in the valley of the shadow, and found me as near to the city's gates as I shall ever be till they open for me; and that is an experience whose influence can never quite depart from a human soul.

To be within touch of the unseen and eternal, to lose one's hold on earth and earthly things, to face a last parting from all that makes life sweet, and then to be restored, is calculated to make one ponder with a new, keen interest the mystery of life and death. The message such restora-tion has to give is undoubtedly that there is still some work remaining here which I, and I alone can do. We cannot shift responsibility nor leave to others the mission to which we are called. Very humble such mission may be, no more perhaps than the sweeping of a room, or the cooking of a daily dinner, but whatever it be let us, as holy George Herbert has it—

"Make that, and the action fine."

Being spared, then, I seek to work more earnestly, to give of my best. Of the added gift which has come to me and mine this precious year, I ought not, perhaps, to say much, though the child naturally occupies so much of my time and thoughts. These few words I may permit myself, because so many whom I shall never see have rejoiced in our joy, sending greeting which has touched us again and yet again. The joy of motherhood is very great, and as yet without alloy. Care comes when the little ones are grown and spread their wings beyond our ken, when we have to take them on trust, staying our hearts with faith and prayer. There are many sad hearts among mothers this Christmas-tide. When I look upon my darling asleep in her cot, with Heaven's seal of innocence and peace yet upon her face, I think of those whose eyes have been gladdened by such innocence and lived to see it made shipwreck of, whose hope is blasted, and who thank God for the little ones beneath the sod. Many of these mothers have been as prayerful, conscientious, and wise as I try so hard to be. Yet is such bitter sorrow theirs. To such compensation must be yonder, since it is not here. And I say to those mourning over the downfall of their hopes this Christmas-tide, that if they will only have faith, nothing wavering, and cast their burden on the Lord, they may yet see the wherefore of much that is hard to understand, and prove that, though weeping may endure for a night, joy cometh in the morning.

And now, having said so much, there o remains for me to bid farewell with my read to the year that has gone. To the many w have given me of their sympathy and encoura ment, I return my thanks. I am glad to thin nay, to know—from many direct sources, t some have found some comfort, stimulus, a enjoyment in these pages. Such assurance coming in from time to time upon a very bu life, give much encouragement, and make labo light. Sympathy, the bond upon which agreed when we met first over the teacups, h never failed between us, and has been help to my readers and to me.

* * *

The older I grow the more strongly do I f that it is not love that saddens the earth, but dearth of it. There is too much living to s among us all; we are too apt to regard the lit world within our own four walls as the only sp of any consequence in the world, and throu such narrow vision we are bound to becor selfish and circumscribed. Let us look beyor The whole human brotherhood should conce us, even as it concerned our Master when walked with men. We want more light, mo wideness of vision, more sympathy to go o from us towards the suffering, the tempted, a the sad. If any are hesitating, not knowing t way wherein to walk, let them read the who duty of man as Christ has given it in the fif chapter of Matthew's Gospel. Let us take the incomparable words for our guide througho the year; then shall life be a lovely, a nob a satisfying thing, a daily sacrifice which G Himself will delight to honour.

HOW DR. DAVIDSON KEPT HIS LAST CHRISTMAS AT DRUMTOCHTY.

BY IAN MACLAREN.

CHRISTMAS fell on a Sunday the year Doctor Davidson died, and on the preceding Monday a groom drove up to the manse from Muirtown Castle.

"A letter, Doctor, from his lordship "—John found his master sitting before the study fire in a reverie, looking old and sad—" and here's a bit boxie in the kitchen."

"Will you see, John, that the messenger has such food as we can offer him?" and the Doctor roused himself at the sight of the familiar hand-writing; "there is that, eh," half fowl that Rebecca was keeping for my dinner to-day; perhaps she could do it up for him. I . . do not feel hungry to-day. And, John, will you just say that I'm sorry that . . . owing to circumstances, we can't offer him refreshment?" On these occasions the Doctor felt his straitness greatly, having kept a house in his day where man and beast had of the best.

"What dis for the minister of Drumtochty an' his . . . hoose ill dae for a room, even though he serve the Earl o' Kilpindie, an' a' ken better than

say onything tae Becca aboot the chuckie;" this he said to himself on his way to the kitchen, where that able woman had put the messenger from the Castle in his own place, and was treating him with conspicuous and calculated condescension. He was a man somewhat given to appetite, and critical about his drink, as became a servant of the Earl; but such was the atmosphere of the manse and the awfulness of the Doctor's household that he made a hearty dinner off ham and eggs, with good spring water, and departed declaring his gratitude aloud.

"MY DEAR DAVIDSON,—Will you distribute the enclosed trifle among your old pensioners in the Glen as you may see fit, and let it come from you, who would have given them twice as much had it not been for that confounded bank. The port is for yourself, Sandeman's '48 —the tipple you and I have tasted together for many a year. If you hand it over to the liquidators, as you wanted to do with the few bottles you had in your cellar, I'll have you up before the Sheriff of Muirtown for breach of trust and embezzlement as sure as my name is

Your old friend,
KILSPINDIE.

P.S.—The Countess joins me in Christmas greetings, and charges you to

'Don't like that signature, Augusta, said the Earl.'

fail us on New Year's Day at your peril. We are anxious about Hay, who has been ordered to the front."

The Doctor opened the cheque and stroked it gently; then he read the letter again and snuffed, using his handkerchief vigorously. After which he wrote:—

"DEAR KILSPINDIE,—It is, without exception, the prettiest cheque I have ever had in my hands, and it comes from as good a fellow as ever lived. You knew that it would hurt me not to be able to give my little Christmas gifts, and you have done this kindness. Best thanks from the people and myself, and as for the port, the liquidators will not see a drop of it; don't believe any of those stories about the economies at the manse which I suspect you have been hearing from Drumtochty. Deliberate falsehoods; we are living like fighting cocks. I'm a little shaky— hint of gout, I fancy—but hope to be with you on New Year's Day. God bless you both, and preserve Hay in the day of battle.— Yours affectionately,

ALEXANDER DAVIDSON."

"Don't like that signature, Augusta," said the Earl to his wife; " it's true enough, for no man has a warmer heart, but he never wrote that way before. Davidson's breaking up, and . . . he 'ill be missed. I must get Manley to run out and overhaul him when he comes down. My belief is that he's been starving himself. Peter Robertson, the land steward, says that he has never touched a drop of wine since that bank smashed; now that won't do at his age, but he's an obstinate fellow, Davidson, when he takes a thing into his head."

The Doctor's determination—after the calamity of the bank failure—to reduce himself to the depths of poverty was wonderful, but Drumtochty was cunning and full of tact. He might surrender his invested means and reserve only one hundred pounds a year out of his living, but when he sent for the Kildrummie auctioneer and instructed him to sell every stick of furniture, except a bare minimum for one sitting-room and a bedroom, Jock accepted the commission at once, and proceeded at eleven miles an hour— having just bought a new horse—to take counsel with Drumsheugh. Next Friday he dropped into the factor's office—successor to him over whom the Doctor had triumphed gloriously—and amid an immense variety of rural information, mentioned that he was arranging a sale of household effects at Drumtochty Manse. Jock was never known

to be so dilatory with an advertisement before, and ere he got it out Lord Kilspindie had come to terms with the liquidator and settled the Doctor's belongings on him for life.

The Doctor's next effort was with his household, and for weeks the minister looked wistfully at John and Rebecca, till at last he had them in and stated the situation.

"You have both been . . . good and faithful servants to me, and I may say . . . friends for many years, and I had hoped you would have remained in the manse till . . . so long as I was spared. And I may mention now that I had made some slight provision that would have . . . made you comfortable after I was gone."

"It wes kind o' ye, sir, an' mindfu'." Rebecca spoke, not John, and her tone was of one who might have to be firm and must not give herself away by sentiment.

"It is no longer possible for me, through . . . certain events, to live as I have been accustomed to do, and I am afraid that I must . . . do without your help. A woman coming in to cook and . . . such like will be all I can afford."

The expression on the housekeeper's face at this point was such that even the Doctor did not dare to look at her again, but turned to John, whose countenance was inscrutable.

"Your future, John, has been giving me much anxious thought, and I hope to be able to do something with Lord Kilspindie next week. There are many quiet places on the estate which might suit . . . " then the Doctor weakened, "although I know well no place will ever be like Drumtochty, and the old manse will never be the same . . . without you. But you see how it is . . . friends."

"Doctor Davidson," and he knew it was vain to escape her, "wi' yir permission a' wud like tae ask ye ane or twa questions, an' ye 'ill forgie the leeberty. Dis ony man in the Pairish o' Drumtochty ken yir wys like John? Wha 'ill tak yir messages, an' prepare the fouk for the veesitation, an' keep the gairden snod, an' see tae a' yir trokes when John's awa? Wull ony man ever cairry the bukes afore ye like John?"

"Never," admitted the Doctor, "never."

"Div ye expect the new wumman 'ill ken hoo mickle stairch tae pit in yir stock, an' hoo mickle butter ye like on yir chicken, an' when ye change yir flannels tae a day, an' when ye like anither blanket on yir bed, an the wy tae mak the currant drink for yir cold?"

"No, no, Rebecca, nobody will ever be so

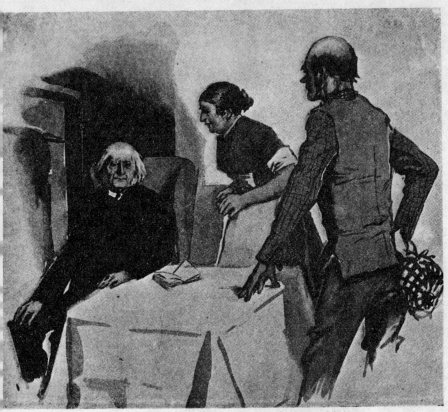

"Wull ony man ever cairry the bukes afore ye like John?"

good to me as you've been "—the Doctor was getting very shaky.

"Then what for wud ye send us awa, and bring in some handless, useless tawpie that cud neither cook ye a decent meal nor keep the manse wise like? Is't for room? The manse is as big as ever. Is't for meat? We 'ill eat less than she 'ill waste."

"You know better, Rebecca," said the Doctor, attempting to clear his throat; "it's because . . . because I cannot afford to . . ."

"A' ken very weel, an' John an' me hev settled that. For thirty year ye've paid us better than ony minister's man an' manse hoose-keeper in Perthshire, an' ye wantit tae raise oor wages aifter we mairrit. Div ye ken what John an' me hev in the bank for oor laist days?"

The Doctor only shook his head, being cowed for once in his life.

"Atween us, five hundred and twenty-sax pund."

"Eleven an' sevenpence," added John, steadying his voice with arithmetic.

"It's five year sin we askit ye tae py nae-thin' mair but juist gie's oor keep, an' noo the time's come, an' welcome. Hev John or me ever disobeyed ye or spoken back a' thae years?"

The Doctor only made a sign with his hand.

"We' ill dae't aince, at ony rate, for ye may gie us notice tae leave an' order us oot o' the manse; but here we stop till we're no fit tae serve ye or ye hae nae mair need o' oor service."

"A homologate that "—it was a brave word, and one of which John was justly proud, but he did not quite make the most of it that day.

"I thank you from my heart, and . . . I'll never speak of parting again," and for the first time they saw tears on the Doctor's cheek.

"John," Rebecca turned on her husband —no man would have believed it of the

"Swooped down upon
him with the dog-cart.'

manse, when the gleb
was let to Netherton
declined to rende
any account to Re
becca, and the Docto
had to take the mat
ter in hand.

"There's a little
business, Mrs. Baxter
I would like to settle
with you, as I happer
to be here." The
Doctor had dropped
in on his way back
from Whinny Knowe
where Marget and he
had been talking o
George for two hours
"You know that I
have to be, eh . .
careful now, and I
. . . you will let me
pay what we owe for
that delicious butter
you are good enough
to supply."

"Ye 'ill surely tak
a look roond the fields
first, Doctor, an' tell's
what ye think o' the
crops;" and after that
it was necessary for
him to take tea.
Again and again he
was foiled, but took
a firm stand by the
hydrangea in the gar-
den, and John Baxter
stood aside that the
affair might be de-
cided in single com-
bat.

"Now, Mrs. Bax-
ter, before leaving I
must insist," began
the Doctor with au-
thority, and his stick
was in his hand; but
Jean saw a geographical advantage, and
seized it instantly.

"Div ye mind, sir, comin' tae this gairden
five year syne this month, and stannin' on
that verra spot aside the hydrangy?"

The Doctor scented danger, but he could
not retreat.

"Weel, at ony rate John an' me dinna forget that day, an' never wull, for we were
makin' ready tae leave the home o' the
Baxters for mony generations, an' it wes you

beadle of Drumtochty, but he was also . . .
"what are ye stoiterin' roond the table for?
it's time tae set the Doctor's denner; as for
that chicken," and Rebecca retired to the
kitchen, having touched her highest point
that day.

The insurrection in the manse oozed out,
and encouraged a conspiracy of rebellion
in which even the meekest people were concerned. Jean Baxter of Burnbrae, who had
grasped greedily at the dairy contract of the

that stoppit us. Ye 'ill maybe no mind what ye said tae me."

"We 'ill not talk of that to-day, Mrs. Baxter . . . that's past and over."

"Aye, it's past, but it's no over, Doctor Davidson; na, na, John an' me wesna made that wy. Ye may lauch at a fulish auld wife, but ilka kirnin' (churning) day ye veesit us again. When a'm turnin' the kirn a' see ye comin' up the road, an' a' gar the handle keep time wi' yir step; when a' tak oot the bonnie yellow butter ye're stannin' in the gairden, an' then a' stamp ae pund wi' buttercups, an' a' say, 'You're not away yet, Burnbrae, you're not away yet'—that wes yir word tae the gude man; and when the ither stamp comes doon on the second pund and leaves the bonnie daisies on't, 'Better late than never, Burn-

"Which Saunders from Drumsheugh . . . had piled on either side."

brae; better late than never, Burnbrae.' Ye said that afore ye left, Doctor."

Baxter was amazed at his wife, and the Doctor saw himself defeated.

"Mony a time hes John an' me sat in the summer-hoose an' brocht back that day, an' mony a time hev we wantit tae dae somethin' for him that keepit the auld roof-tree abune oor heads. God forgie me, Doctor, but when a' heard ye hed gien up yir glebe ma hert loupit, an' a' said tae John, 'The'll no want for butter at the manse sae lang as there's a Baxter in Burnbrae.'

"Dinna be angry, sir," but the flush that brought the Doctor's face unto a state of perfection was not anger. "A' ken it's a leeberty we're takin', an' maybe a'm presumin' ower far, but gin ye kent hoo sair oor herts were wi' gratitude, ye wudna deny us this kindness."

"Ye 'ill lat the Doctor come awa noo, gude wife, tae see the young horse," and Doctor Davidson was grateful to Burnbrae for covering his retreat.

This spirit spread till Hillocks lifted up his horn, outwitting the Doctor with his attentions, and reducing him to submission. When the beadle dropped in upon Hillocks one day, and, after a hasty review of harvest affairs, mentioned that Doctor Davidson was determined to walk in future to and from Kildrummie Station, the worthy man rose without a word, and led the visitor to the shed where his marvellous dog-cart was kept.

"Div ye think that a' cud daur?" studying its general appearance with diffidence.

"There's nae sayin' hoo it wud look wi' a wash," suggested John.

"Sall, it's fell snod noo," after two hours' honest labour, in which John condescended to share, "an' the gude wife 'ill cover the cushions. Dinna lat on, but

Wednesday when the Doctor went to Muirtown to buy his last gifts to Drumtochty, he was very cunning, and ran the blockade while Hillocks was in the corn room, but the dog-cart was waiting for him in the evening — Hillocks having been called to Kildrummie by unexpected business—and it was a great satisfaction afterwards to Peter Bruce that he placed fourteen parcels below the seat and fastened eight behind —besides three which the Doctor held in his hands, being fragile, and two, soft goods, on which Hillocks sat for security. For there were twenty-seven humble friends whom the Doctor wished to bless on Christmas Day.

When he bade the minister good-bye at his gate, Hillocks prophesied a storm, and it was of such a kind that on Sunday morning the snow was knee deep on the path from the manse to the kirk, and had drifted up four feet against the door through which the Doctor was accustomed to enter in procession.

"This is unfortunate, very unfortunate," when John reported the state of affairs to the Doctor, "and we must just do the best we can in the circumstances, eh?"

"What wud be yir wull, sir?" but John's tone did not encourage any concessions.

"Well, it would never do for you to be going down bare-headed on such a day, and it's plain we can't get in at the front door. What do you say to taking in the books by the side door, and I'll just come down in my top coat, when the people are gathered;" but the Doctor did not show a firm mind, and it was evident that he was thinking less of himself than of John.

"A'll come for ye at the usual 'oor," was all that functionary deigned to reply, and at a quarter to twelve he brought the gown and bands to the study—he himself being in full black.

"The drift 'ill no tribble ye, an' ye 'ill no need tae gang roond; na, na," and John could not quite conceal his satisfaction, "we 'ill no start on the side door aifter five and thirty years o' the front."

So the two old men—John bare-headed, the Doctor in full canonicals and wearing his college cap—came down on a fair pathway

"We must soon . . . depart."

a'll be at the gate the morn afore the Doctor starts," and Peter Bruce gave it to be understood that when Hillocks convoyed the Doctor to the compartment of the third rigidly and unanimously reserved for him, his manner, both of walk and conversation, was changed, and it is certain that a visit he made to Piggie Walker on the return journey was unnecessary save for the purpose of vain boasting. It was not, however, to be heard of by the Doctor that Hillocks should leave his work at intervals to drive him to Kildrummie, and so there was a war of tactics, in which the one endeavoured to escape past the bridge without detection, while the other swooped down upon him with the dog-cart. On the

etween two banks of snow three feet high, which Saunders from Drums-
eugh and a dozen plowmen had piled on either side. The kirk had a
vere look that day, with hardly any women or children to relieve the
lackness of the men, and the drifts reaching to the sills of the
indows, while a fringe of snow draped their sides.

The Doctor's subject was the love of God, and it was noticed
at he did not read, but spoke
s if he had been in his study.
e also dwelt so affectingly
n the gift of Christ, and made
 tender an appeal unto his
eople, that Drumsheugh blew
is nose with vigour, and Hil-
cks himself was shaken.
fter they had sung the para-
hrase,

To Hm that lov'd the souls of
        men,
    And washed us in His blood,"

e Doctor charged those
resent to carry his greetings
 the folk at home, and tell
em they were all in his
eart. After which he looked
 his people as they stood for
 least a minute, and then
ting his hands, according to
e ancient fashion of the
cottish Kirk, he blessed
em. His gifts, with a
ecial message to each per-
n, he sent by faithful mes-
ngers, and afterwards he
ent out through the snow to
ake two visits. The first was
 blind Marjorie, who was
ree Kirk, but to whom he
d shown much kindness all
er life. His talk with her
as usually of past days and
untry affairs, seasoned with
holesome humour to cheer
er heart, but to-day he fell
to another vein, to her great
elight, and they spoke of the
ispensations of Providence.

"'Whom the Lord loveth,
e chasteneth,' Marjorie, is a
ery instructive Scripture, and
was thinking of it last night.
ou have had a long and hard
ial, but you have doubtless been blessed,
r if you have not seen outward things, you
ve seen the things . . . of the soul." The
octor hesitated once or twice, as one who
d not long travelled this road.

"You and I are about the same age,
arjorie, and we must soon . . . depart.

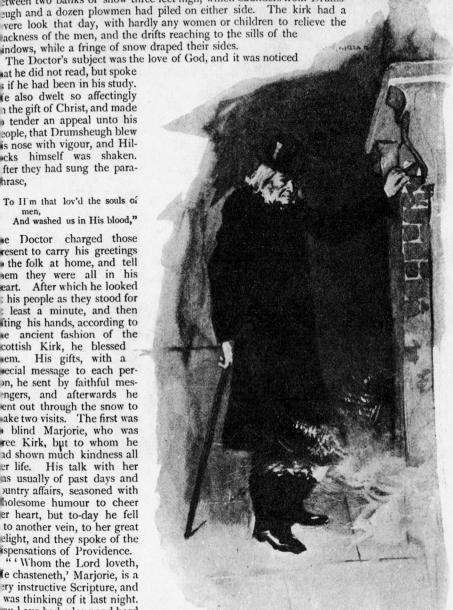

" And a gust of wind coming down the vast open chimney
powdered his coat with drift."

My life was very . . . prosperous, but lately
it has pleased the Almighty to . . . chasten

me. I have now, therefore, some hope also that I may be one of His children."

"He wes aye gude grain, the Doctor," Marjorie said to her friend after he had left, "but he's hed a touch o' the harvest sun, an' he's been ripening."

Meanwhile the Doctor had gone on to Tochty Lodge, and was standing in the stone hall, which was stripped and empty of the Carnegies for ever. Since he was a laddie in a much-worn kilt and a glengarry bonnet without tails, he had gone in and out the Lodge, and himself had seen four generations —faintly remembering the General's grandfather. Every inch of the house was familiar to him, and associated with kindly incidents. He identified the spaces on the walls where the portraits of the cavaliers and their ladies had hung; he went up to the room where the lairds had died and his friend had hoped to fall on sleep; he visited the desolate gallery where Kate had held court and seemed to begin a better day for the old race; then he returned and stood before the fireplace in which he had sat long ago and looked up to see the stars in the sky. Round that hearth many a company of brave men and fair women had gathered, and now there remained of this ancient stock but two exiles—one eating out his heart in poverty and city life, and

"Drumsheugh dined with the Doctor that night."

a girl who had for weal or woe, God only knew, passed out of the line of her traditions. A heap of snow had gathered on the stone, where the honest wood fire had once burned cheerily, and a gust of wind coming down the vast open chimney powdered his coat with drift. It was to him a sign that the past was closed, and that he would never again stand beneath that roof.

He opened the gate of the manse, and then, under a sudden impulse, went on through deep snow to the village and made a third visit—to Archie Moncur, whom he found sitting before the fire reading the *Temperance Trumpet.* Was there ever a man like Archie?—so gentle and fierce, so timid and fearless, so modest and persevering. He would stoop to lift a vagrant caterpillar from the cart track, and yet had not adjectives to describe the infamy of a publican; he would hardly give an opinion on the weather, but he fought the drinking customs of the Glen like a lion; he would only sit in the lowest seat in any place, but every winter he organised—at great trouble and cost of his slender means—temperance meetings which were the fond jest of the Glen. From year to year he toiled on, without encouragement, without success, hopeful, uncomplaining, resolute, unselfish, with the soul of a saint and the spirit of a hero in his poor, deformed, suffering little body. He humbled himself before the very bairns, and allowed an abject like Milton to browbeat him with Pharisaism, but every man in the Glen knew that Archie would have gone to the stake for the smallest jot or tittle of his faith.

"Archie," said the Doctor, who would not sit down, and whose coming had thrown the good man into speechless confusion, "it's the day of our Lord's birth, and I wish to give you and all my friends of the Free Kirk—as you have no minister just now—hearty Christmas greeting. May peace be in your kirk and homes . . . and hearts.

"My thoughts have been travelling back of late over those years since I was ordained minister of this parish and the things which have happened, and it seemed to me that no man has done his duty by his neighbour or before God with a more single heart than you, Archie.

"God bless you." Then on the doorstep the Doctor shook hands again and paused for a minute. "You have fought a good fight,

" Ye never heard o' God, Skye."

rchie—I wish we could all say the same . . . a good fight."

For an hour Archie was so dazed that he was not able to say a word, and could do nothing but look into the fire, and then he turned to his sisters, with that curious little movement of the hand which seemed to assist his speech.

"The language wes clean redeeklus, but wes kindly meant . . . an' it maks up for mony things. . . . The Doctor wes aye a gentleman, an' noo . . . ye can see that he's . . . something mair."

Drumsheugh dined with the Doctor that night, and after dinner John opened for them a bottle of Lord Kilspindie's wine.

"It is the only drink we have in the house, for I have not been using anything of that kind lately, and I think we may have a glass together for the sake of Auld Lang Syne."

They had three toasts, "The Queen," and "The Kirk of Scotland," and "The friends that are far awa," after which—for the last included both the living and the dead—they sat in silence. Then the Doctor began to speak of his ministry, lamenting that he had not done better for his people, and declaring that if he were spared he intended to preach more frequently about the Lord Jesus Christ.

"You and I, Drumsheugh, will have to go a long journey soon, and give an account of our lives in Drumtochty. Perhaps we have done our best as men can, and I think we have tried; but there are many things we might have done otherwise, and some we ought not to have done at all.

"It seems to me now, the less we say in that day of the past the better. . . . We shall wish for mercy rather than justice, and "—here the Doctor looked earnestly over his glasses at his elder—"we would be none the worse, Drumsheugh, of a friend to . . . say a good word for us both in the great court."

"A've thocht that masel"—it was an agony for Drumsheugh to speak—"mair than aince. Weelum MacLure wes . . . ettlin' (feeling) aifter the same thing the nicht he slippit awa, an' gin ony man cud hae stude on his ain feet . . . yonder, it wes . . . Weelum."

The Doctor read the last chapter of the Revelation of St. John at prayers that evening with much solemnity, and thereafter prayed concerning those who had lived together in the Glen that they might meet at last in the City.

"Finally, most merciful Father, we thank Thee for Thy patience with us and the goodness Thou hast bestowed upon us, and for as much as Thy servants have sinned against Thee beyond our knowledge, we beseech Thee to judge us not according to our deserts, but according to the merits and intercession of Jesus Christ our Lord." He also pronounced the benediction—which was not his wont—and he shook hands with his two retainers; but he went with his guest to the outer door.

"Good-bye, Drumsheugh . . . you have been . . . a faithful friend and elder."

When John paid his usual visit to the study before he went to bed, the Doctor did not hear him enter the room. He was holding converse with Skye, who was seated on a chair, looking very wise and much interested.

"Ye're a bonnie beastie, Skye "—like all Scots, the Doctor in his tender moments dropped into dialect—"for a'thing He made is verra gude. Ye've been true and kind to your master, Skye, and ye'll miss him if he leaves ye. Some day ye'll die also, and they 'ill bury ye, and I doubt that 'ill be the end o' ye, Skye.

"Ye never heard o' God, Skye, or the Saviour, for ye're juist a puir doggie; but your master is minister of Drumtochty, and . . . a sinner saved . . . by grace."

The Doctor was so much affected as he said the last words slowly to himself that John went out on tiptoe, and twice during the night listened—fancying he heard Skye whine. In the morning the Doctor was still sitting in his big chair, and Skye was fondly licking a hand that would never again caress him, while a miniature of Daisy—the little maid who had died in her teens, and whom her brother had loved to his old age —lay on the table, and the Bible was again open at the description of the New Jerusalem

MY MOST MEMORABLE CHRISTMAS.

I.

NOTHING happened the Christmas I spent at Fort Ross, on the northern coast of California; but it is the only Christmas that I can summon up on a moment's notice, nevertheless. I think it was a bright day, and that the roses were blooming; but nothing could be more monotonous than life at Fort Ross at any time, for it is a small hamlet on the cliffs, sixty miles from anywhere. I had to send to San Francisco for wrapping-paper and twine for my MSS. But there was a time when Christmas was a great festival at Fort Ross, in the days when Europe had barely heard the name of California, when the Russians of the Alaska Fur Company, disregarding the protest of the Spaniards, had seized a great tract on the northern coast, and when a princess was in exile there. All this was before 1842, when the Russians, having exhausted the otters, went away. Since then the property has passed through various hands, including those of Charles Fairfax of Virginia, at that time the head of the only family in the United States holding a British title—Baron of Cameron—though he never used it, of course. He was once governor of California, and a brilliant, dashing, reckless person, about whom many anecdotes still linger. The Miss Christian Fairfax who is about to make her *début* here as a singer belongs to the same family. But all this is by the way.

The Russians, although they knew they had nothing to fear from the indolent Californians, dreaded the hostility of neighbouring Indian tribes, and fortified themselves very strongly. The fort was drawn up in the form of a square with bastions at two corners and mounted cannon in the courtyards. The barracks and one end of the governor's house faced the Pacific; the back of the enclosure was set against the lower slope of the mountain, on whose top began a redwood forest. Outside, and on an adjoining cliff, were huts accommodating some eight hundred Indians and convicts, servants of the Company. At one corner of the fort was a church, magnificently decorated within; tradition says there was a jewelled altar. The Company was a very wealthy one, and the governors—who were gentlemen, and doubtless regarded themselves as exiles—took every luxury with them. The last governor, Alexander Rotscheff, whose bride, the Princess Hélène, followed him willingly into exile, fitted up his big log-house so sumptuously that he could draw the blinds and forget the desolate cliffs and the black forests where panthers cried and lions roared; as well as the indignant tribes beyond. Once only were they actually threatened with an Indian invasion, and, if I may be allowed, I will quote the incident from a former story.

"It happened only the other day. Prince Solano, perhaps you have heard, is chief of all the tribes of Sonoma, Valley of the Moon. He is a handsome animal, with a strong will and remarkable organising abilities. One day I was entertaining the Rotscheffs at dinner, when Solano suddenly flung the door open and strode into the room. We are old friends, and my servants do not stand on ceremony with him. As he caught sight of the Princess, he halted abruptly, stared at her for a moment, much as the first man may have stared at the first woman, then turned and left the house, sprang on his mustang, and galloped away. The Princess, you must know, is as blonde as only a Russian can be, and an extremely pretty woman, small and dainty. No wonder the mighty prince of darkness took fire. She was much amused. So was Rotscheff, and he joked her the rest of the evening. Before he left, however, I had a word with him alone, and warned him not to let the Princess stray beyond the walls of the fortress. The same night I sent a courier to General Vallejo—who fortunately was at Sonoma—bidding him watch Solano. And, sure enough, the day I left for Monterey, the Princess Hélène was in hysterics, Rotscheff was swearing like a madman, and a soldier was at every carronade. Word had just come from General Vallejo that he had that morning intercepted Solano in his triumphant march at the head of six tribes, upon Fort Ross, and sent him flying back to his mountain-top in disorder and bitterness of spirit."

Naturally I became very much interested in the Princess Hélène, and learned all I could about her. The Rotscheffs only remained two or three years, and I fancy the pretty Russian was rather bored, despite the attentions of her big clever husband, and hastened their departure. Once in a while the gay Californians, in *reboso* and flowered silks, velvet smallclothes and silver-laden sombreros, galloped over from the Fort and Mission of Sonoma and danced for a night or two ; but with one tragic exception she had no visitors from home, and was dependent for the society of her own sex upon the wives of the officers guarding her lonely home. I only met one person who had actually seen her—a gnarled old Indian woman with the brownest skin and the whitest teeth I ever saw. She described the Princess to me with a good deal of minuteness, and told me that she used to sit in the porch doing nothing most of the time. In the evenings she often played for Rotscheff, and she rode with him occasionally. On Sundays she and her husband and all those associated with them went up to the orchard near the forest and lunched there, looking down on the ocean and listening to the murmur of the redwoods, sometimes to sounds more menacing. Christmas was a great festival, and she usually managed to have several Californians as guests. A great swing was erected among the cannon ; and the Princess, who had loved her Paris, seemed to take a childish delight in being sent high by her husband's strong arms. Games of every sort were played in the courtyard, and dancing kept up till dawn. Out on the cliffs the working men also had a holiday ;

Indians and convicts wrestled amicably, and played all the games they knew or could invent. Once a man wrestled with his wife on the edge, and she went over and was drowned. He received the benefit of the doubt, and as he had detested her, doubtless passed a happy Christmas.

People at Fort Ross vow that on very dark and stormy nights they hear moans down on the beach, supposed to emanate from the ghosts of rebellious convicts, who were executed by the governors' orders ; and shrieks from the ruins of an old grist mill on a hill beyond the fort. I stayed there four months, and never heard anything but the wind, which blew my window in one night, and threatened to carry the rocking wooden structure, built on to the end of the old loghouse, straight over the cliffs into the ocean ; but I longed to hear those ghostly sounds, and was much interested in the yarns which fathered the superstition. A beautiful Russian, Natalie Ivanhoff, is said to have come on a visit to the Princess, and, in spite of prohibition, to have insisted upon taking long walks on the cliffs by herself. One day she came face to face with a convict—in whom, in spite of a terribly altered exterior, she recognised the lover whom she had mourned for several years. Much agitated, she returned to the house, not observing that she was followed by the miller's son, an ugly youth whose open admiration had caused her some annoyance. After several days' delay, and with the help of a neighbour, she made arrangements for the flight of herself and her lover : they were to meet at the mill, which was deserted at midnight, then mount the horses which were awaiting them in the forest, and fly to Monterey, where they would be hidden and protected by the Californians. In spite of sharp-eyed sentries, Natalie managed to escape from the Fort and made her way to the mill. Once she fancied herself followed, and paused to listen ; but the footfalls ceased with her own, and the fog was so dense she could see nothing. In the mill her lover awaited her, and so absorbed were they in each other's society for a moment that neither heard stealthy steps in the adjoining room. Then there was a sudden and hideous end to love and

"Stared at her for a moment, then turned and left the house."

hopes. Natalie, whose heavy hair was unbound, was standing with her back to one of the band wheels; the machinery, without warning, began to revolve, her hair was caught and she was whirled upwards and crushed before her horrified companion could get into the next room. He flung himself over the cliffs, and what was left of her was placed in a copper coffin—made from ships' plates—and buried on the bare knoll which stands prominently between the ocean and the forest. I used to wander about this burying-ground, with its fifty or so trodden graves marked only by a high rough wooden cross, and try to settle satisfactorily in my mind which was the grave of Natalie Ivanhoff. But if it had ever been marked the wood had rotted long since.

They also tell the story of a convict who attempted to escape, was caught, and made to walk the plank one Christmas morning from a Russian man-of-war, then anchored off the cliffs. He is also supposed to join in the chorus of the storm, but I listened for him in vain.

Fort Ross in my time—some eight years ago—was a sort of tavern, very comfortable and, as I was the only boarder, an ideal spot for a writer; not only on account of its romantic memories, but because of its wild beautiful surroundings. There was a store-post-, telegraph-, express-office near by, and a farm in sight; and all the lions and bears are gone long since. The beautiful Princess Hélène is old or dead, and would be forgotten but for a great peak which her husband formally named for her—Mount St. Helena. My only companion was a little girl of nine who used to accompany me on my walks and, although a young person of ideas and much independence of character, never opened her lips except when I spoke to her. I never had a more sympathetic companion. Her name was Lucille. Once I asked her who she was named for: it was a romantic name to find in the wilderness. "Oh," she replied, with some impatience, "after that book." Thus had the fame of "Owen Meredith" penetrated even into the loneliest spot I have ever known.

IV.

AN EVENTFUL CHRISTMAS, SIXTY-FIVE YEARS AGO.

BY G. B. STUART.

"YOU think that nothing happened in our young days," said the Very Old Lady, "and that we lived stupid, humdrum lives without interest or adventure; whereas I can tell you——"

We hastened to assure her that we thought nothing of the kind, and were longing to hear her story, and presently, after a little coaxing, she began her annual Christmas recital.

"My father, who had a large family, and loved shooting and a country life, had taken a rambling old château in Holland during the minority of the Count to whom it belonged; he found living there much cheaper

than in England, and we had occupied it already for several years when the division of Holland and Belgium into two separate kingdoms caused us to question to which side of the newly established frontier we really belonged.

"Papa did not meddle in politics, and treated Dutch and Belgians alike. All the same he had once in the worst of the winter entertained some passing Dutch troops with food and beer, and some of our Maestricht neighbours said this was unwise of him; but he always replied that he would give the Belgians the same when they wanted it!

"Meanwhile, Christmas was upon us, and we were full of our home preparations for the festival. Besides our own family of parents, boys and girls, our only visitor was Mr. Kupfers, our tutor from the village of Gulpen, who had hinted broadly to be invited to spend the day and take part in the English Church Service which papa always read on Sundays and Feast-days to the assembled household ; we suspected that his keen desire to perfect himself in English prompted the little man's religious zeal.

"Anyway, he arrived quite early, before ten o'clock on this bright frosty Christmas morning, bringing a present of gingerbread and gilded walnuts in his canvas bag. Adeline and I entertained him in the schoolroom till papa and mamma should have finished their breakfast ; while the boys kept out of sight, for they considered Mr. Kupfers unnecessary on a holiday !

"Our schoolroom had, like all the other ground-floor rooms, long French windows opening on the courtyard. Suddenly, as we sat chatting politely, these windows were darkened, and the clatter of arms and rough Belgian voices filled all the terrace with a rude clamour. We crowded to look out, and there was a surly-looking sergeant with some forty men at his back parleying with papa, who had come out on the dining-room steps to ask their business. Apparently he satisfied them, for the men all settled down in attitudes of expectancy about the courtyard, and Jacob the steward brought out beer and tobacco to which they helped themselves freely. 'Some of them have had enough beer already,' observed Kupfers ; 'they are Belgian militia who ought to have gone home long ago ; they have heard how your honoured father treated the Dutchmen, and have come to try his hospitality too ! Heaven grant they take themselves off without damage !'

"An uneasy hour passed, and it was time for our Christmas Day Service. Papa came out again, and spoke to the sergeant, who answered with scant politeness that his men needed rest and a good meal of meat. Under cover of ordering a meal to be prepared for them papa despatched Jacob for assistance to Gulpen, for he began to guess that matters were growing serious. Jacob could run to the village in half an hour, and be back in another with a stout band of our country neighbours to the rescue.

"'No Church Service this morning, I fear,' said Mr. Kupfers with a sigh. We opened the schoolroom door to listen and peep, and heard papa's voice giving a hurried order to Alice, our nurse : 'Get your mistress and the children and the young maids up to the attic as fast as you can ; then you and Jeanne and Peter come and help me feed these ruffians, and make the business last as long as you can, so as to give Jacob time to return !'

"We stood horror-struck at the gravity of papa's tone, and Alice's unusually brief 'Yes, sir !' A moment later she had swept us all out of the schoolroom and up the servants' staircase to the attic, a long, low loft right under the rafters, where old boxes and lumber were stored. We longed to stay below where we could see and hear what was going on, but should as soon have thought of attacking the forty militia men single handed as of disobeying Alice, and up the attic stairs we tumbled, mamma and the boys with two younger maids joining us from another wing of the great house.

"Alice counted us as we stood in the dusty sunshine of the loft ! 'Good Lord ! where's baby ?' she cried, and darted off as if she had been shot from a gun. Mamma, who was nervous and delicate, sat down, all trembling, on an old packing-case. 'O my baby, my baby !' was all she could say ; but in a trice Alice was in our midst again, holding baby upside down in her arms. 'There she was, the precious, sitting up in her chair, and calling for her Nannie ! Sure she was her Nannie would not long forget her !'

"'Did you see Mr. Kupfers, Alice ?' we asked anxiously.

"'No,' snapped Alice, 'I'd other fish to fry,' and she bounced off as mamma locked the door behind her. 'We're rid of poor little Kupfers,' whispered Adeline, 'but what's the good of a holiday if we're to be locked up here all day ?'

"I don't remember that we were frightened at first. By crawling on a pile of boxes we could watch the movements in the court below ; and presently all the invaders entered the house by the dining-room windows. 'Alice has found food for them,' suggested mamma ; 'there is plenty in the larder—hares and partridges, bacon and cheese, and yesterday's baking of bread. If they will sit down to table it will be all right, for very soon now Jacob must be back from Gulpen with assistance. Look out down the avenue and see if any one is coming.'

"'No, madame,' answered Marie, the nursery maid, who commanded the window. 'I can see as far as the high road, but there is no sign of Jacob; only two little figures that go up and down like sentries.'

"The second hour was much longer than the first; we were all growing hungry, the boys were squabbling faintly, and baby woke up crying; mamma was looking pale, and the silence below tried her nerves. We had not seen papa pass for some time. We all jumped when a tap came at the door. 'It's me, Alice! open quickly!' and there was Alice, sure enough, the door safely relocked behind her.

"'Here's the beef, ma'am!' she panted. 'I didn't let them have it, the dirty brutes, but I fear it's burnt to a coal. I've been serving those scoundrels with the best, and I just whipped the sirloin into the oven till I could slip away with it, and some milk for my precious! Here, Marie, see if you can cut up the beef. Master Jack's sure to have a knife in his pocket!'

"This was to be our Christmas dinner! 'Where's your master?' mamma asked.

"'Trying to keep order among them ruffians, as are drinking his best wine and smoking his fine cigars—they are all best part drunk now, and some are asleep on the sofas,' said Alice.

"'But Jacob should be back by now.'

"'Yes, ma'am dear, so he ought.' But Alice spoke so dubiously that Adeline and I cried out together, 'Do you think he has been stopped? There are sentries at the gate; Marie saw them!'

"'Master can't be sure, so now he has sent Peter to Maestricht on the mare for the soldiers to come. He went by the wood to avoid being seen, and if he got safe away he ought to have done half the ten miles by this time.'

"'O Alice,' interrupted mamma, 'do you mean that your master is the only man left among that dreadful crew?'

"'Don't you be afraid. I'm going back to him,' said Alice valiantly. 'Young ladies and gentlemen, if you've finished your meat wipe your fingers and say your grace, for it's Christmas pudding you'll get to-day, I'm afraid!'

"We hated to see Alice go, for she was our one link with the excitement below. 'What do you think has become of poor little Kupfers?' whispered Adeline. 'If he tried to run away perhaps they've hamstrung him, like the Ancients used to do. I wish I'd learnt my Latin better.'

"'Don't be silly,' I said, for I was afraid she was going to have one of her sentimental crying fits. 'Nobody hamstrings nowadays; and if they hurt little Kupfers they'd all be hung, because he's a Government official and a non-combatant, you know.'

"'And if they shot papa?' Jack asked.

"'If they hurt a hair of his head all England would come to chop Belgium and Holland to mincemeat,' said I, choosing a Christmas simile; 'for papa has been a British Dragoon Captain!'

"And now a very dismal time set in. Our first excitement was over, and the grey dusk of the December afternoon began to settle down. The boys were snappish and fidgety, and one of the maids whined and sniffed in an irritating fashion. Mamma spoke bravely of there being no danger, but her voice faltered, and she wondered papa had not been upstairs to reassure us. We little guessed how serious things had become downstairs. Suddenly the gloom below was lighted up, and from the window I saw a drunken figure stagger across the courtyard, carrying the two Dresden china lamps from the drawing-room, their wicks flaming half a yard high. As he set them down on the wall the globes shivered to a thousand pieces, but by their glare I could see that the work of devastation was in full swing. Men were dragging out the furniture and ornaments of the château, and piling it as for a bonfire. I watched to see if papa would appear; surely he and Alice must have been struck down before they could have permitted such wholesale destruction of the Count's property committed to their care! Darker grew the night, but the Dresden lamps flared like two

"We crowded to look out."

beacons, and the crowd of black forms was thick round them.

"'Fire the house!' came up in a howl of fury, and immediately a shaft of flame burst out of the centre pile of household stuffs.

"'What is that?' cried mamma, starting from a half doze; 'are they going to burn us like rats?' and she flew to the door and tried to unlock it with shaking fingers.

"But even at that moment, apart from the din below, my ears caught the sound of advancing cavalry. 'Well done, Peter!' I shouted, leaping up and down in my excitement; 'we're saved! we're saved! Here are the troops from Maestricht!'

"I could not see much more, for in the wild scrimmage that followed the lamps on the wall were knocked over; the rioters were all mad with drink, and the Regulars easily mastered them.

"Alice came rushing upstairs to fetch us down to the nursery, beyond which none of us, not even mamma, were allowed to go—I guessed from Alice's voice and manner that not the wounded alone lay below. She brought wine and bread to feed us, and stirred up the great stove. As we crouched round it we heard papa's voice in the corridor, and mamma dashed out to meet him. It was many, many years afterwards that she told me she had believed him dead all that dreadful afternoon.

"'Don't tell it at home,' said papa, 'that a Captain of Dragoons and his maidservant hid together in the straw of the stable! But though Alice is as good as five ordinary men, that only made us six against forty! Two of the rascals came and dug at us with pitchforks; but their hands were not oversteady, and the Count's good claret had sapped their determination! Now, children, to bed, to bed! This long Christmas Day has come to an end for you at least; but don't forget when you say your prayers to thank God for keeping us all safe in a time of great danger!'

"Next morning a carriage came to take us away to Maestricht. I shall never forget the scene in the courtyard as we started—burnt and broken furniture littered the terrace, and the stones were stained with dark marks, while under the wall lay a row of stiff, straight forms under a couple of horse-blankets. Mamma hastily moved the little boys that they should not face the silent, solemn row!

"Then as the doors were banged, some one came rushing up, waving his hat and a parcel of dingy books, and thrust his head into the carriage window. It was Kupfers, alive and smiling! 'My dear, my honoured young ladies, keep these and study assiduously till in happier times we meet again!' he exclaimed, and then the horses bounded away.

"Mamma was laughing almost hysterically and wiping her eyes. 'When you were all in bed,' she said, 'and I went at last to my room, I could not get the door of my big Almira to open. I pulled and pulled, and at last called Alice to help, and lo! from the inside of the hanging wardrobe crept poor little Kupfers, almost imbecile with cold and fright. To-day he has recovered, and I daresay he thinks he fought with the best!'

"'I said he was a non-combatant,' said I.

"Papa, mamma, and all the rest have gone before me," concluded the Very Old Lady; "but there is the story of an eventful Christmas nearly seventy years ago. Thank God, children, for peace and goodwill in your times!"

MISS BARTRAM'S EXPERIMENT.

By Annie S. Swan.

ISS BARTRAM was very plain and very unattractive, and occasionally very cross. Yet people said that she had almost everything in the world she could wish for. Certainly she was rich, and she lived in a splendid house surrounded by acres of grounds, laid out in the most delightful ornamental fashion. But as she herself often said, she had not a living soul in the world to care whether she lived or died—except for the legacies which she was supposed to be going to leave to her various relatives. She had a good many relatives of one kind and another—chiefly cousins, who took a great deal of interest in her because of her money. She did not trouble to make herself agreeable to them, so that perhaps it would have been too much to expect them to care for her; yet she had been very kind to most of them, though they had shown but little gratitude. Miss Bartram had grown a little tired of it all, and one day in December of a certain year, which Miss Bartram's relatives have much cause to remember, a strange idea struck her. She was sitting at one of the long windows of her great drawing-room, looking out upon the lawn, on which the white flakes of the first snow-storm were softly falling, and she felt very miserable, and lonely, and sad. Christmas was at hand, and it meant little to her but the expenditure of a good deal of extra money in the purchase of Christmas gifts for her large circle of relatives. Then she was expected to ask as many as lived at a convenient distance to dinner at The Cedars on Christmas Day, and somehow Miss Bartram had a feeling that the whole thing was hollow and insincere. She was rather a shrewd, clever, old lady, and she did not believe that among all those who shared her bounty there was one who took a real

interest in her or had any love for her in their hearts; and suddenly a great desire took possession of her to try them, to discover whether among them all there might be one disinterested soul. She got up with a look of quiet exultation on her face, and rang the bell with an undecided hand.

"Tell Ringold I want the carriage in half an hour to drive to Market Bainton," she said sharply; and in half an hour, accordingly, she drove away through the softly falling snow to the county town, which was only three miles distant. The carriage, by her order, was stopped at the office of Geoffrey Hendon, the solicitor, in County Square; and Miss Bartram alighted and went in.

Geoffrey Hendon was an old friend of hers and had managed her affairs for years. He knew all she had done for her relatives, he also knew that they did not regard her with either respect or esteem; but he had never hinted at this, nor allowed her to say it even. He was a kindly soul; and he had seen so much of dissension in families that he was for ever on the side of peace.

"This is rather a bitter day for you to venture out, Miss Bartram," he said cheerily as he set a chair for her near the bright fire. "I feel this weather myself. We are not getting any younger, eh—and old blood feels the frost of years."

"Quite true, friend, but I did not notice the weather in my comfortable brougham. Well, it's nearly Christmas again."

"I've been expecting a visit from you," said the lawyer with a nod, Miss Bartram having always been in the habit of consulting him about her Christmas distribution. "What's the programme this year?"

"Quite a new one, Mr. Hendon," she replied, with a smack of her thin lips which betrayed a good deal of satisfaction. "I'm not going to bestow any Christmas cheer this year; I am going to seek it."

"What do you mean?" asked the lawyer, looking at her with a puzzled air, noting her elation, and wondering what was at the bottom of it.

Soon she enlightened him.

"I'm tired of giving, Mr. Hendon. I'm going to try the blessedness of receiving for a change. Will you help me?"

"You'll need to explain yourself first," observed the lawyer with his customary caution.

"Well, I'm going out into the world to spend Christmas, a poor woman."

"How can you do that?"

"Oh, I must pretend a little. That's what half the world is doing anyhow. I must say my riches have taken wings. I can't do it, of course, without your assistance."

"Do you mean to say you'll tell all your relatives, the Gillmans, the Lees, the Bartrams, and the Fawcetts, that you have lost your money, Miss Bartram?" exclaimed the lawyer in amazement.

"That's precisely what I do mean, Mr. Hendon. Then I'll find out who are my real friends; you'll not deny that."

"You may; but it's a dangerous experiment which you may regret. I should advise you not to try it."

"Oh, but my mind is made up, my good man. If you won't help me, promise me not to betray me, at least."

"Oh, I can hold my tongue, if you mean that. It's no temptation to me to speak. Are you going to write to them and tell them this odd fabrication?"

"Yes, this very night. I'll write to every Gillman, Lees, Fawcett, and Bartram among them, telling them I have had terrible reverses, and that I shall have to turn out of The Cedars : surely some of them will offer me a home, or ask me to spend Christmas, at least."

"Oh, I have no doubt the Gillmans will, seeing you've kept Bertie at Oxford for

"He set a chair for her near the bright fire"

two years," said the lawyer drily. "But it doesn't seem right; it's telling a downright lie, you know, and the Bible says we may not do evil that good may come."

"Don't you preach to me, Geoffrey Hendon," said the old lady tartly. "I am quite willing to answer for my own sins. I think the Gillmans will be all right, and the Bartrams too, for they are my own flesh and blood—I don't expect much from the Lees or Fawcetts, but we'll see. Good day. I'll write those letters to-night, and bring the replies to let you see them, though you don't deserve it. The Araminta Mines would do, wouldn't it?"

"What for?"

"A convenient pit to sink my gold in for a time," she said, with a twinkle in her eye."

"It will do as well as anything else, Miss Bartram," said the lawyer. "But mind, I neither sanction nor approve of it, and if you get your fingers burnt over it, don't blame me."

"That's all right: don't you worry over me," said Miss Bartram, as she bade him an amiable good-bye.

They were friends of a lifetime, and had frequent bickerings, which scarcely ruffled the good understanding between them.

"I fear Miss Bartram is getting into her dotage, Ben," observed Mr. Hendon to his son as he watched the carriage out of sight.

But the old lady was very lively; as excited over her new idea as a child over its latest toy. That very evening the harrowing epistles to her relatives were written and despatched, and in due time Mr. Hendon received a second visit from his rich client.

As more than a week had passed since the last visit, he had come to the conclusion that she had thought better of it. He gathered something different from her face, however, the moment she entered his room.

"Well, I've done it. I've found them all out," she said shrilly—almost vindictively. "Now tell me first, have you had a visit from Tom Gillman and George Lees, my nephews?"

"They called here one morning, I believe, but I was at Warwick, at the assizes."

"Well, I had a call from them pretty sharp, I can tell you. Tom was the most upset, and he had the cheek to ask what was the lowest price I would take for The Cedars, and said his wife would call and select what articles I might be disposed to sell cheap."

The lawyer tried to conceal his amusement, for he saw that Miss Bartram was feeling hurt and sore.

"But what about Christmas? Did any of them offer you the Christmas cheer you wanted?"

"Oh, I've brought the letters; they'll convince you if nothing else will," said Miss Bartram, fumbling nervously with the silver clasps of her old-fashioned velvet reticule. "There is only one Christian letter in the pack, but it'll do your heart good to read it."

"Who wrote it?"

"Why, my niece, Nina Bartram, who married John Fawcett against my will. I've never seen her since. Read that—look—and tell me what you think of it."

Mr. Hendon took the dainty little envelope from Miss Bartram's hand, and perused it from beginning to end.

> "WITLEY END, WORCESTERSHIRE,
> "*Dec.* 15*th.*

"DEAR AUNT BARTRAM,—We were much upset to receive your letter containing such distressing news. It is very sad for you; but perhaps when everything is wound up you will not be quite so badly off. John has told me to write you at once, and ask you to come to us for Christmas, and as long as you like. Then we can talk everything over. If only you would make a friend of John, dear aunt, you would never regret it. He is so clever, and everybody trusts him. We have prospered beyond our expectations, and as every Christmas you have kindly remembered us it is our turn to remember you. If you don't like children I can give you a room where you will scarcely hear their noise, and though I have a new baby, she is so good we scarcely know we have her, except for our joy. Now, dear aunt, don't hesitate, but come at once. John will meet you at Birmingham and bring you out, or will even come all the way to Oldcote if you will let him. If you won't accept our invitation, then we must come to see you. With love and sympathy,

"Your affectionate Niece,
"NINA FAWCETT."

"The letter of a kind woman and a good woman, Miss Bartram," said the lawyer. "And she is quite right about her husband. I know that John Fawcett is beginning to be known in the iron world."

"Well, then, perhaps you want to read the others just as a wholesome tonic. Mary Gillman says they have no spare room, as the house is filled with Bertie's school friends, and the Bartrams have the measles, and George Lees and his wife are going into Suffolk to spend Christmas with her mother; so it's Stourbridge or nothing."

"I should certainly advise you to go there," said the lawyer heartily. "You've caught the others nicely, and though I can hardly say they don't deserve it, I feel sorry for them."

"Sorry for them indeed!" quoth the old lady in high scorn. "They'll be sorry for themselves one of these fine days. I shall never forgive Tom Gillman coming sneaking round to see whether he could buy my house cheaply over my head. But he has overreached himself this time; I shall never believe his cry of poverty again."

A few days later Miss Bartram left The Cedars, giving all the servants a holiday, and departed to Birmingham, very plainly attired and carrying but a small quantity of luggage. She was in high glee, but also felt slightly nervous, for it was something of an ordeal to visit on such terms at the house of the niece whose marriage with a working-man, as she had termed him, had angered her so deeply. She arrived at New Street about four o'clock in the afternoon, and popping her head out of the window she saw the stalwart figure of John Fawcett waiting for her on the platform. She thought him much improved since she had seen him last, almost fifteen years before. He was a fine, handsome, happy-looking person with a face which at once inspired trust. He caught sight of her presently, and came forward, raising his hat.

"How do you do, Miss Bartram? I am very glad to see you. Nina would have come too, but baby was troublesome last night and I persuaded her to stop and take a rest, so that she would be bright and like herself when you arrived."

"You are very kind, John Fawcett, and I have never deserved it at your hands," said the old lady gruffly. He only smiled, carefully assisted her to alight, and took all her numerous wraps on his arm. Very soon he had her comfortably settled in the Stourbridge train, and as the carriage was very full they got small opportunity of talking during the short journey. When they got to their destination there was a cab awaiting them, into which John again handed the old lady carefully.

"We hope to have a carriage some day, Miss Bartram, but not yet awhile. There's a grand opening at our works just now; I only wish I could take it."

"What is it?" she asked sharply.

"One of the younger partners has died, and his share is to be sold. They offered it to me, and I could have had twenty years to pay it in; but I didn't see my way, and Nina thought we should be better plodding along quietly."

"No, John; I don't know that. Big ventures pay. How much do they want for it?"

"Oh, I shouldn't like to tell you—a matter of ten or twelve thousand, I believe. Well, here we are; it isn't a long drive, and there's Nina at the door."

At this the old lady began to tremble violently, and her eyes filled with unwonted tears; for there was nothing but loving-kindness and compassion on her niece's sweet face as she came running to meet her. Although she was now the mother of five children she scarcely looked a day older.

"Welcome, Aunt Bartram; we are all very glad to see you. Here are all the children ready to tell you so."

They all came crowding round her, making quite a little fuss, and yet all so kind and gentle that poor Miss Bartram was almost overcome, and felt like telling them on the spot that she was nothing but a fraud. When Nina took her up to the pretty guest-chamber with its bright fire, and showed her

at the little hands had done to make it
eerful for her—Lucy's cherished Christmas
se on the dressing-table, and Dick's poker-
rk table which he had made for his
other, and of which he was inordinately
oud—the lonely old woman felt more and
ore ashamed; for she had often thought
d said hard things of these simple homely
rd-working people who had thought the
orld well lost for love; and here they
ere the true gold after all.

Space forbids me to chronicle the events
the next few weeks, or to describe the
anner in which Christmas was spent at
itley End. It was a pretty old-fashioned
use, and in the field behind the house
ere was a glorious duck-pond where the
ung Fawcetts enjoyed themselves im-
ensely during the frost. They even
rsuaded Aunt Bartram to try on a
ir of skates, and she
came astonishingly
volous and happy, so
at often her niece re-
rded her with amaze-
ent. She could scarcely
lieve this humble-
inded, amiable woman,
ateful for every small
rvice rendered, to be
e same grim, sour,
mineering one she had
own in her early days.

"The uses of adversity
ve been sweet to Aunt
artram, John," said Nina
her husband one night
ter they went upstairs.

"She is certainly most amiable,
ar," John answered. "Have you
ought what is to become of her
there is so little left as she ex-
cted?"

"I have thought of course that
might be our duty to ask her
remain here," said Nina, with a
gh; "but I am so afraid to spoil
e children's happiness. You know
have always agreed that we ought
make them as happy as possible
w, because of the troubles we
nnot bear for them later."

"But the children are devoted to her,
Nina, and she to them."

"Just now, John; but it might be a
different matter if she were always here.
Then there are all the other relatives. The
Gillmans are much better off than we are."

"But they won't have her, dear. You
heard her say so. Don't forget that she is
your aunt, dear, and was kind to you once.

" The harrowing epistles to her relatives were written.

"They all came crowding round her."

Besides, she is a sad, lonely old woman, without any friends."

"O John, I do think you are the best man in the whole wide world," cried Nina, as she threw her arms round his neck. "And to think that she ever dared to think you were not good enough for poor little me! I'll speak to her to-morrow."

Nina Fawcett slept soundly that night with the happy consciousness of duty shared and a kind act about to be done. Next morning, after John had gone to business and the children off to school, it being now the second week in January, Nina opened the

conversation with the old lady, as she sat contentedly in the most comfortable chair by the fire.

"Aunt Bartram," she said, a trifle nervously, "John and I were talking of you last night, and if things should turn out as badly as you expect, we shall be very glad if you will come here and make your home with us; we will do our best to make you happy. I don't think you mind the children as I feared you would."

Miss Bartram did not speak a word, but Nina saw the large tears coursing down her cheeks.

"' Behind the house was a glorious duck-pond, where the young Fawcetts enjoyed themselves immensely during the frost."

"I have not deserved this from you, ina," she said at length. "I can't think hat you and John are made of. You rtainly are too good for this world."

"Oh, dear no," said Nina brightly; "only ry ordinary folk. Well, shall we say it's ttled? And you can have the room in the uth gable you like so much, and while you

are gone back to Oldcote to gather your things together I shall have it nicely papered and painted for you."

"I am going away to-morrow, Nina, but don't do anything to the south room until you hear from me. Though I should never come to occupy it permanently, I shall always regard it as mine : I have uttered a great many grateful prayers in it."

Nina wiped her eyes, and coming to her aunt's side, kissed her affectionately.

Next day Miss Bartram insisted on departing, and everybody was sorry, even the servants, to whom, forgetting for a moment the *rôle* she was playing, she presented a sovereign each. She promised to write without fail next day, and accordingly on the second morning the letter came, addressed, somewhat to Nina's surprise, to her husband instead of herself.

"She is trying to make up to you, John," she said, nodding brightly across the table. "Never mind, I am not a bit jealous."

John opened the letter, which did not appear to be very long, and as he unfolded it saw a slip of paper which looked uncommonly like a cheque.

"I hope the old lady hasn't sent a cheque for her board," he said, with a laugh; but as he unfolded it his face paled a little. "Why, Nina, what's the meaning of this? A cheque for twelve thousand pounds!"

"Read the letter,

John; it will explain. Surely Aunt Bartram can't be quite right in her head."

This was the letter to which the family circle listened in breathless amazement:—

"THE CEDARS, OLDCOTE,
"*Jan. 4th.*

"MY DEAR, DEAREST NEPHEW AND NIECE,—I have to begin by humbly apologising for playing a trick on you, but it will be easily explained, and, I hope, forgiven. A lonely, miserable, selfish old woman got it into her head that there were no such things as love or kindness or generosity in this world, and she made up her mind to test the whole matter for herself. So she made pretence that her riches had taken wings, and went forth into the world to see some Christmas cheer for herself. Among all those to whom she had tried to be kind in her own grudging selfish fashion she found only one family who would show her any consideration and these she had treated worst of all. Oh, my dears, God bless you for what you have done, you have opened my eyes, and made me believe in God again and in the

"Nina . . . coming to her aunt's side, kissed her."

goodness of my kind. That is a service which can never be paid for, just as I can never, never thank you for your sweet kindness. It has made a different woman of me. If John refuses to accept what I send—the money to buy the partnership—it will break my heart. It is only anticipating matters a little, for in any case you would have that at my death. So please write or come if you can and tell me you forgive your foolish but happy old aunt,

"KATHARINE BARTRAM."

"A fairy tale, mother," said gentle Lucy

eagerly ; but neither John nor his wife spoke a word. They were afraid to look at each other, their hearts were so full. That very day they went to Oldcote, and everything was settled. Aunt Bartram still lives, and divides her time equally between Witley End and Oldcote.

As for the other relatives, they have not heard the outs-and-ins of the story to this day ; but believing Miss Bartram's money affairs to be in a shaky condition, they hold themselves a good deal aloof.

Miss Bartram smiles when she thinks how wide they will open their eyes one day.

COOKERY.

MENU FOR A CHRISTMAS DINNER.

Menu.

Celery Soup.
Cod à la brème.
Boned Quails.
Boiled Turkey.   Mushroom Sauce.
Brussels Sprouts au Jus.
Roast Round of Beef.
Ox Tongue à la Belgravia.
Christmas Pudding.   Wine Sauce.
Mince Pies.   Orange Sponge Jelly.

CELERY SOUP.

Two quarts of veal stock, boiled with six heads of celery, strain, and add more celery cut very fine, and two ounces of butter mixed with three tablespoonfuls of flour. Stew till the celery is quite tender, and just before removing from the fire add half a pint of cream previously scalded. Season with salt, pepper, and a little sugar.   Cost, 2s. 6d.

COD À LA BRÈME.

Put into a stewpan a good piece of butter, half a spoonful of flour, a clove of garlic minced fine, and some whole pepper; moisten with milk or cream, thicken the sauce on the stove. Put in the fillets of cod and serve very hot. Cost, Cod 1s.   Ingredients, 1s.

BONED QUAILS.

Bone the birds without opening—that is, work the knife from the neck.   Roll in buttered paper after trussing, and bake on a buttered tin in a brisk oven.   Dish whole on a rice block or border.   Mask with good brown sauce, flavoured with a little sherry.   Cost (three quails), inclusive, 3s. 6d.

MUSHROOM SAUCE.

Chop about a pound of veal and half a pound of ham in small pieces; add a dozen mushrooms, two onions sliced, cloves, mace, herbs, and a quarter of a pound of butter. Let all stew gently in white gravy for an hour and a half.   Mix one pint of cream with half a teacupful of flour, and add it to the stock.   Boil up, strain, and season with salt and pepper. Cost, meat 10d.   Stock, 1s. 2d.

BRUSSELS SPROUTS AU JUS.

Boil for a few minutes in water, then stew till tender in good gravy, seasoned with salt and pepper.   Toss them in a frying pan with a little butter—do not let them brown.   Serve with white sauce.   Cost, inclusive, 7d.

OX TONGUE À LA BELGRAVIA.

Cook gently for three hours or more, according to size.   Boil in vegetable stock—clear—and when done tie up the tongue, trim and skin it, brush over with glaze, and pour round the dish a little brown sauce, and garnish with tomatoes (cooked).   Cost, about 6s.

CHRISTMAS PUDDING.

Four ounces of bread crumbs, $\frac{1}{2}$ lb. of muscatel raisins (stoned), 1 oz. of flour, 1 lb. of sliced kidney suet, $\frac{1}{4}$ lb. of powdered sugar, $\frac{1}{2}$ lb. of picked and washed currants, salt, mixed spice, candied lemon peel, the rind of two, and the juice of one, lemon.   Beat six eggs with some new milk and a glassful of brandy.   Mix all well together and let it stand two or three hours.   Boil for five hours briskly.   Cost, 2s. 4d.

ORANGE SPONGE JELLY.

Dissolve 2 oz. of isinglass in 1 pint of water, and strain through a sieve.   Add the juice of two China oranges, four Seville oranges and one lemon, with about $\frac{1}{2}$ lb. of fine sugar; whisk it till it looks like a sponge, put into a mould and leave to set.   Cost, 1s. 2d.

COST OF DINNER.		£	s.	d.
Soup, Fish and Game.	...	0	8	0
Turkey, Beef and Tongue.	...	0	17	6
Vegetables and Sauces.	...	0	2	7
Sweets.	...	0	5	0
		£1	13	1

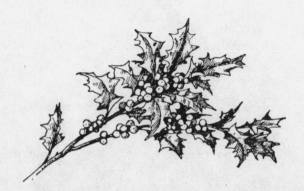

THE

STRAND MAGAZINE

An Illustrated Monthly

EDITED BY

GEORGE NEWNES

Vol. XVIII.

JULY TO DECEMBER

London:

GEORGE NEWNES, LTD., 7, 8, 9, 10, 11, & 12, SOUTHAMPTON STREET,
AND EXETER STREET, STRAND

1899

Christmas Crackers.

F there is one thing inseparable from Christmas in general and the little ones' seasonable gatherings in particular, it is —a cracker. With what a delightful look of expectation they have waited for it to go "bang," and how they have screamed as they scrambled after the surprise which came in response to the explosion, and revelled in a complete outfit in the way of paper garments, hats and caps, jewels, toys, puzzles, and what not. But there are others who love the cracker. Have you not seen them? She is merry eighteen, and he with just enough moustache to twirl. They each seize an end of that convenient little cracker— "bang" it goes. Why doesn't he pick up the gaily decorated paper cap, or she the piquant little apron with the blue bows? Simply because there is a tiny slip of paper inside, and they are eager to read it. That little scrap of paper may say:

"The sweet crimson rose
with its beautiful hue
Is not half so deep as my
passion for you.
'Twill wither and fade,
and no more will be
seen
But whilst my heart lives
you will still be its
queen!"

and the next mo-

ment they are in the quietest corner of the room. It was Cupid himself who hopped out of that cracker. Christmas crackers have much to answer for.

Considering the many moments of merriment which these small rolls of paper will surely bring, and the countless chats

"BANG."

on courting topics they are sure to give rise to, we are inclined to hasten from romance to reality, and take a peep in upon the workers whose busy fingers provide the crackers—in short, to find out exactly how they are made, from the moment the paper arrives at the factory to the time the completed article is ready to be packed up in dozens and sent away. Messrs. Tom Smith & Co., of Wilson-street, Finsbury, are really the creators of the Christmas cracker as we now know it. About forty years ago a sweetmeat and love-motto was wrapped in a piece of fancy paper, and in those days answered the same purpose as Christmas crackers do now. They were called " Kiss Mottoes." Then it got converted into "Somebody's Luggage," and finally got up Christmas Cracker of to-day. Oscar Wilde did much, however, for its welfare. Even the crackers caught the æsthetic movement and became wrapped up in æsthetic colours. Messrs. Tom Smith & Co. manufacture eleven millions in a single season. Our own country will claim some eight or nine millions of these, and the remainder will get scattered over the world, India claiming a big parcel.

The first room visited at their immense factory was on the ground floor. Here is a miniature quarry. Hundreds of stones imported from Germany are stacked everywhere. Men are busy in the far corner grinding and grinding them until a perfectly pure and level surface is obtained. If you feel inclined you might endeavour to raise from the floor the largest litho stone used. It measures sixty inches by forty, and would turn the scale at a ton. The stones are then passed on to the litho artists, for lithography plays a most important part in the manufacture of a Christmas Cracker. Upstairs is the artists' room. Clever artists are constantly engaged in making fresh designs year in and year out, and it is nothing extraordinary for some of them to spend weeks in completing a single set of designs. The literary work, too, is no small

item, and a man who can write good verse can earn good money. Ladies seem to be the most adept at this sort of thing, which is paid for at so much a set of verses. Mr. Walter Smith, who accompanied us on our tour, goes to a desk and takes out a handful of sheets on which all sorts and conditions of bards have written. Some of them are very funny. Here is one, which is immediately waste-paper basketed :—

" Whilst sweets are eaten, and crackers cracked,
  Naughty boys are sure to be whacked."

The poet asked five shillings for this, and offered to supply them in unlimited quantities at the same price.

The next one is a gem, and is at once accepted :—

" Half hidden 'neath the spreading leaves,
  A purple violet bent its head ;
  Yet all around the moss-grown path
  In love its fragrance softly shed.
  My living violet, whisper low,
  That o'er my life your fragrance sweet
  Will make a garden of my life,
  Where love its counterpart may meet ! "

We now pass through innumerable avenues of Christmas crackers, all in huge parcels. In one stack alone there are no fewer than 50,000 boxes in a line one hundred feet long and ten feet wide.

"GRINDING LITHOGRAPHIC STONES."

This represents a month's work, and every one is sold. We can quite realise this when we are told that one retail firm alone in London will send in such an order for crackers that it would take sixteen of the largest delivery vans built to convey them, with 1,200 boxes packed away in each van. It is no unusual thing for an order of £500, £1,000, or £1,500 worth of Christmas crackers to be received, the biggest of all totalling up to £3,000, the highest in the trade. This reminds us of the number of cardboard boxes which must be needed. The box-making is a distinct industry. A plant of machinery for their manufacture costs anything between £2,000 and £5,000, and during

THE PARCEL DEPARTMENT.

a busy week 30,000 would be made and used in that time. The card is all cut to shape and stacked away, and the patterns are many, for there are over 150 varieties of boxes. Just look at this pile of sacks in the corner. It is all waste cuttings, and often ten and fifteen bags will come down the lift in the course of a day.

On the floors above, the printing is going on. A number of litho machines are running, for the most part presided over by men assisted by girls, who certainly take off the sheets with marvellous rapidity. One machine is printing funny faces to go outside the crackers, another is turning out sheets with hundreds of flowers on it, and yet another is giving us countless little Cupids. Every rose and Cupid is cut out, and it is the same with any other picture with which it is intended to decorate a cracker.

We shall be safe in saying that the contents of crackers come from every part of the world, and a peep into the store-room where they are kept in huge bins and great boxes, will substantiate this. On one corner of the counter are thousands of tiny pill boxes. These are filled with rouge and powder,

PRINTING MASKS.

with a little puff thrown in. Such are the contents of one of the " Crackers for Spinsters," those estimable single ladies also being allotted faded flowers, a night-cap, a wedding ring, and a bottle of hair dye. This pile of bracelets came from Bohemia, fans from Japan, toys from Christiania, with little wooden cups and saucers from the same place, scarf-pins from Saxony ; the little miniature pipes, as played on by the accompanist to a Punch and Judy show, are made by Parisians ; Jews' harps come from Germany, and tiny wooden barrels from America. The familiar flexible faces which can be squeezed and pulled into every conceivable shape are made in London. Hundreds of little glass bottles are here, supposed to be filled with a certain intoxicant known as gin. A young girl is filling

Turkey, India, China, and South Africa all contribute to the store. The sight would set a child pining with pardonable envy to play about this part of the factory.

To enumerate every item which

"FROM ALL QUARTERS OF THE GLOBE."

finds its way inside the crackers would call for a catalogue the size of THE STRAND MAGAZINE.

We are now on our way to the top of the building where the Christmas cracker is really made. First, there is the giving-out counter. Here come the girls and receive into their hands a certain quantity of what is wanted to make the particular part on which they are engaged. Every strip of paper is counted. Close by the giving-out counter a number of young women are fringing the edges of the paper to be rolled. This is done on a small machine capable of taking four thicknesses of ordinary paper and six of the brighter-looking gelatine. The material to be fringed is put against the teeth of the apparatus, the girl stamps it, and it is ready to give a neat and gay appearance to either end of the body of the cracker.

The main workroom presents a busy sight. It is nearing one o'clock, when the dinner bell will ring, and the hands are

them with the very reverse of anything intoxicating, although the label on the bottle says " A 1,000,000 overproof." Italy,

FRINGING.

we were watching said she could roll two dozen "best work" in a quarter of an hour, though she could do commoner work much quicker. Her next door companion was blessed with busy fingers. First she took a slip of paper—this was the inner lining ; round this she wrapped the gelatine, added two decorating ends or fringes, and then put in the detonator, the explosive paper tape, and it was ready to receive its contents. She could do a gross an hour. Her fingers travelled faster than the pencil in our note-book. Passing girl after girl, we find them all surrounded by the brightest of colours in gelatine and paper. One is making paper dresses for a doll, a neat little white tissue frock trimmed with red braid. This formed part of rather a novel box of crackers. A good-looking doll is placed in the box, and each cracker has some article of attire inside, so that when every one was "pulled" the doll could be provided with a complete outfit. Others were making hats and caps. The paper is rolled round a tin to shape, pasted together, and there is your *chapeau.* All is very simple, but nothing could be more effective when the article is completed.

The cardboard alone used in the manufacture of the empty boxes in which the crackers are packed exceeds a hundred tons in weight during a single season, and the tiny strips of card constituting the detonators over five tons. Twenty tons of glue and paste, between 6,000 and 7,000

working at high speed so as to finish their self-allotted task ere the bell tolls. Four hundred feet of benches are ranged from end to end of the room, and here are scores of girls sitting in front of partitioned-off spaces ranged along the lengthy counters. Every girl has her glue-pot by her side. Turn round and look at the immense stove where twenty pots are being constantly warmed up, so that as soon as a worker's glue cools down she has only to cross to the stove and there is another pot ready at hand for her. It is noticeable how cheerful the young women are and to what a superior class they apparently belong. A good cracker hand can easily earn 14s., 16s., and at a busy time 18s. a week, and the cracker trade of this firm alone means the constant employment, directly and indirectly, of close upon 1,000 people.

One young woman is rolling the paper — paper of all the colours of the rainbow are before her, and dozens of completed crackers are arranged in front waiting to be carried away, and the manufacture of them booked to her credit. The paper is rolled on a brass tube, so that a trim appearance is obtained. Coloured string ties it up, and the gelatine is quickly placed round it. The girl

CUTTING THE PAPERS.

reams of coloured and fancy papers are used, whilst the total weight of the thin transparent sheets of coloured gelatine, which add so much to the brilliancy of a Christmas cracker, amounts to nearly six tons.

The process by which gelatine is manufactured is a most interesting one. The raw gelatine comes over in five hundredweight casks from Switzerland. It arrives on these shores in thick, rough sheets, measuring six feet by three feet, weighing

MAKING CRACKERS.

about three to four ounces each. It is then reduced to a liquid by steam power; water being added, it is clarified, and while in its liquid state dyes of the richest hues are poured in to render it of the shade of colour desired. While the gelatine is thus in a liquid form, it is poured upon frames of glass, measuring twenty - four inches by eighteen inches, much resembling

window panes. Workmen, by the movement of the glass, allow the melted gelatine to spread over it, and so form a sheet of uniform thickness. These sheets of glass are then arranged in stacks, and the film of gelatine allowed to set. When the gelatine sheets are hard upon the glass, they are then transferred to a room in which a strong current of air is allowed to pass in and out, to complete the drying process. This takes from twelve to eighteen hours, after which a knife is run round the edges of the gelatine, which then being cut with a knife peels easily off the glass, and is now ready for use.

We were curious to know what was the biggest cracker ever made. Crackers are made three feet long, containing a full-sized coat, hat, collar, frill, whiskers, umbrella, and eye-glass. A story is told of a well-known

MAKING CAPS.

size, and when he heard it, exclaimed:

"Three feet! Not big enough for me. Just you order me three dozen crackers, each six feet long!"

The six feet crackers were made and delivered. Whether the nobleman congratulated himself on the fact that he had obtained the largest cracker up to date we do not know, but the biggest of all was that made every night for Harry Payne as clown to pull with the pantaloon in the pantomime at Drury Lane. It was seven feet long, and contained costumes large enough for the merry member of the aristocracy who entered a couple to put on, and a multitude of West-end shop one day and saw one of crackers, which were thrown amongst the these gigantic crackers. He inquired the children in the audience.

CHRISTMAS in the Forest.

A Story for Children.   From the German.

THE little house that, like a lamb strayed from the flock, lay far behind the other houses in the village, belonged to Master Andrew. The house as well as the trade had descended through three generations. Andrew was a shoemaker, like his father and grandfather, and on his father's death had married a peasant maiden.

Alas! for Andrew, another shoemaker settled in the village. He had learnt his craft abroad, and was far more skilful than our villager. Andrew's trade departed, and he was glad to gain a scanty livelihood by patching shoes for the peasants.

Want pressed sorely on the little household, especially as there were six little mouths to feed. But poverty did not drive out peace or happiness. The boys and girls grew up strong and rosy. George, the eldest, helped his father, and was quite clever at putting in a patch. Katie assisted her mother. The younger children brought wood from the forest, and were useful in many ways.

Christmas was approaching. The snow lay thick on the ground. In Andrew's house there were no Christmas preparations. Father and son plied their trade by the feeble light of the oil lamp. The girls sat spinning beside their mother. The younger children, in charge of the second boy John, sat round the hearth cracking nuts.

Andrew whistled softly while the mother told the listening children how Christmas was celebrated in the town, of the fair with its thousand attractions and beautifully decorated fir-trees.

Then Andrew exclaimed: "There are

135

hundreds of firs outside ; perhaps the forester will let us cut down some to sell."

The family applauded the idea. Early next morning Andrew sought the forester, and soon returned, bringing the written permission.

"Quick, boys," cried he, "run and ask your cousin the miner to lend us his large hand-sledge."

Away ran George and John. Their father sharpened the large axe whilst the mother prepared the breakfast. The boys quickly returned with the sledge, and, breakfast over, set out with their father for the forest.

Heavily bent the snow-laden branches ; still and awesome was the white, silent forest; weirdly rose the old, black tree-trunks from out the white landscape surrounding them ; bravely the three toiled through the deep snow.

At length Andrew halted before a spot where stood innumerable dwarf firs that seemed to grow expressly for Christmas-trees. The strokes of an axe were heard and a little tree fell, shaking the snow from its dark green branches. Gleefully the boys placed it in the sledge. A second followed.

"Give me the axe, father ; let me try," cried George. His father handed it, and with skilful strokes the boy felled the third tree. "Listen, father," he continued ; "there is plenty of work waiting you at home, and very little time to finish it. You go home ; I will fell the trees while Jack loads the sledge. When it is full we will return."

His father agreed. "Be careful," said he ; "the axe is sharp. And do not overload the sledge !" Then he left them.

"Do not stay late !" he called, looking back.

"Very well, father," cried George, with uplifted axe.

Warmed by their work, the boys heeded neither wind nor snow. The fallen trees breathed forth a fragrant perfume ; their ice-bound branches drooped sorrowfully as though grieving to leave their forest home.

Their work ended, the boys harnessed themselves to the sledge and started for home. Just as they regained the tall fir George stopped, exclaiming : "The axe !"

Yes, the axe ! It had been left behind. They could not return without that. A moment George hesitated ; then he said : "Wait a bit, Jack. I will run back for the axe. I know just where it is."

Away he ran, calling as he went : "Stay with the sledge, Jack."

Jack watched till he was out of sight ;

then, weariness overpowering him, he sat down on the sledge. Pushing the branches aside, he saw something shine. It was the axe ! Seizing it, he ran after his brother calling : "George ! George !" No answer. He turned slowly back and seated himself on the sledge with the axe on his lap.

Meanwhile, George searched anxiously but found no axe. Darkness crept on, and with heavy heart he returned to the sledge. John was still there, but he had fallen asleep. The axe lay in the snow. George picked it up, then shook his brother, but, to his dismay, Jack would not wake. He half opened his eyes, muttered some unintelligible words, and then fell back asleep. George let him sleep, and tried to draw the sledge by himself ; but it would not stir.

Anguish and terror now overcame the poor boy. What could he do ? Where obtain help ? He feared Jack would be frozen. Suddenly a light shone in the distance. He ran towards it, and found to his astonishment that it proceeded from the old, ruined castle. He climbed to the window, and the strange sight that greeted him made him for a moment forget his trouble.

In the centre of the hall burned a large fire ; over it was a vat-shaped vessel that sent forth spicy odours. All around hundreds of tiny forms were working busily. On one side sat many little men, some sewing garments of glittering tissue, others making beautiful little shoes. And they worked so swiftly. Husch ! husch ! a coat, cap, or shoe was finished, and flew away to the piles of garments standing beside the little workers.

At the farther end of the hall, cooks were making cakes, which, when baked, they carried two by two on small white boards to a hole in the wall that evidently led to the dwarfs' store-cupboard. Two little men, mounted on stones, stirred the vat with long wands.

"They will certainly enjoy their Christmas," thought George, sniffing the spicy odours.

But a new-comer appeared. He was also a dwarf, but different from the others in dress and appearance. He wore a green hunting-dress made from the wings of earth-beetles ; a hat of like colour adorned his head ; his hair and beard were long. At his side hung a gold hunting-horn. Majestic he stood amidst the workers, who saluted him respectfully. Raising his eyes, he beheld the intruder, and his glance was one of anger.

George sprang down, but, quick as lightning, the gnome climbed through the opening and stood before the terrified boy. The same moment the fire was extinguished, the bustle ceased, and the castle stood silent and dark in the snowy forest.

"How dare you spy out our secrets?" cried the angry little man.

George raised his fur cap. "Honoured sir," said he, "I came not to spy, but to implore your aid."

His politeness soothed the enraged gnome; he inquired the cause of distress, and when told, said: "Lead me to the sledge. I will see if I can help you."

George ran quickly forward, followed by the little man, and soon reached the sledge. John still slept. His face and hands were icy cold. In terror George shook him. Raising his horn, the gnome blew a long, shrill blast, and instantly gnomes arose from behind every tree, mound, and bush.

He gave his commands in a strange, lisping speech. The gnomes hastened away, but speedily returned with a jug, which they handed to their lord. Mounting the sledge, the gnome poured its contents between the lips of the sleeping boy, who immediately

"THE GNOME POURED ITS CONTENTS BETWEEN THE LIPS OF THE SLEEPING BOY."

awoke, and stared wonderingly at the strange company.

George quickly explained what had happened, adding that he owed his life to the gnome's kind care. John thanked the little

man, and declared he never felt better in his life.

Then the gnome questioned them about their family, and learning that they would have no Christmas rejoicings, bade them bring their brothers and sisters to the old castle and join the gnomes' Christmas feast.

The boys joyfully agreed and, thanking him for his kind invitation, turned to depart.

"Stay," said the gnome; "mount the sledge and hold each other tight!" He then ordered his servants to drag them to the last tall fir. The boys mounted. A hundred gnomes harnessed themselves to the sledge, and away they went, swift as the wind. That was a ride! They had barely started ere their father's house was in sight; the sledge stopped, and the gnomes vanished. As they clambered down their father came towards them.

"How could you stay so late?" he asked. "Your mother is very anxious and vexed that I left you."

They entered the cottage. Supper was ready, but they could eat nothing until they had related their strange adventure. Their father shook his head.

"Yes, yes," said he, "I knew the gnomes haunted the old castle, but I have never seen them; still, George is a Sunday child, and might well see things that are hidden from others."

"Of course, they must go," said the mother, "or the little people will be angry and do us harm."

The following morning Andrew, with a horse and cart borrowed from the miner, drove his Christmas-trees to the town. All the children ran out to see the cart loaded, and when it drove away they followed. Passing through the village, other children joined them, forming quite a procession.

At the end of the village Andrew stopped, saying, "Run back to school now, children; and you, George, make haste with your mending." The little crowd turned back, and the cart with its green burden went briskly forward.

Reaching home, George worked industriously for some hours. Then shouts and laughter attracted him. He looked out. Beneath the tall fir the school-children were heaping up the snow.

"Ah, a snow-man!" he exclaimed. "I must help!" Away flew the boot with its half-finished patch, and away sped the little cobbler to join the laughing throng. Merry were the workers and loud their shouts as George, mounted on his shoemaker's stool, placed the snow - man's head upon his shoulders; and there the giant stood, tall and threatening as a winter god.

Then the children joined hands and danced round him, singing merrily, heedless of the icy blast that blew sharply against their laughing faces. Soon George returned to work; the others ran back to school, and his frozen Majesty stood solitary and forsaken.

When the moon rose behind the forest, bathing the snow-clad world in her silver light, George's boot had long been finished, the shoemaker slept beside his sleeping family, and in the box with the Sunday clothes lay a little leather purse filled with silver coins that he had brought back from the town.

The longed-for night arrived, and at the first blast of the golden horn that was to summon them to the feast, the children, dressed in their Sunday clothes, hastened to the forest.

Beneath the tall fir they paused in amaze. The snow-man reared his hoary head on high. But on his arms and shoulders, and on every branch of the fir, sat the gnomes who had come to guide their little guests through the forest.

Climbing swiftly down, they tripped lightly before the children. Gaily the girls' red frocks fluttered above the white snow; merrily the silvery laugh of the children rang through the silent forest.

When they reached the castle it was ablaze with light, whilst all around the tall firs, like giant Christmas - trees, were bright with various coloured stars.

They crossed the threshold to the sound of a million tinkling bells. Within all was light and glittering splendour. The ground and walls were covered with soft green moss, spangled with violets cut from amethysts and sapphires, whilst the carnations and snowdrops glistening between were cut from rubies and pearls, their tiny leaves shedding forth rays of dazzling light. A large sun, formed of carbuncles and diamonds, shed over all a light brighter than day. The children believed it a real sun and the flowers real flowers. Beneath stood a gigantic fir, its topmost branches almost touching the sun, and seeming every moment as though they would burst into flames. Showers of sparks fell from the sun and, resting like stars on every needle-pointed leaf, there sparkled and glittered.

On the branches hung every imaginable fruit, from the tiniest berries to the golden pineapple, all made and moulded with exquisite skill of sugar-pastry; no confectioner could have fashioned them more beautifully than had the little fingers of the gnome-cooks. All around fluttered butterflies, dragon-flies, and cockchafers, whom the gnomes had woke from their winter sleep, and who, placed in this beauteous garden, believed that spring had really come, and dived into the petals of the glittering flowers or stole the sweetness from the sugar fruits.

The children moved about on the tips of their toes, holding each other's hands, and murmuring, "How beautiful! Oh, how beautiful!" Their guides had departed, and save for the butterflies and cockchafers they were alone. The stillness and splendour almost took away their breath.

Strains of sweet music broke the silence; nearer and nearer it came, louder and louder it swelled, as, two by two, a train of little musicians in glittering doublets, blowing and fiddling on tiny instruments, passed through a slit in the wall and formed a circle round the tree.

Little men with long beards followed, and after them came the King, in whom George recognised his friend with the golden horn. Beside him walked the Queen, closely veiled. Both wore gold mantles ornamented with precious stones, and had crowns of fame on their heads. Next came many old men in gold robes. These wore red caps, and were evidently ministers of state, they looked so grave and thoughtful.

Then followed shining carriages drawn by rats and moles. In these sat the gnome ladies, all veiled. A gnome coachman sat on each carriage, and a gnome footman stood behind.

The King and Queen ascended a mossy eminence, on which stood two gold thrones. The ladies alighted from their carriages, which drove slowly away.

Then the King made a long speech. The children could not understand a word, but it must have been very touching, for many of the ladies, and even the beautiful little Queen, wept with emotion.

The speech ended, the musicians broke forth into joyous strains, the gnomes sported merrily, and grove and grotto re-echoed with gay laughter.

"THE PROCESSION."

The King approached the children and asked kindly how they liked it. At first, respect for the gold mantle, the crown, and the speech, kept them silent; but at length George stammered forth : "It is beautiful above measure, beautiful as Heaven!"

Meanwhile the cooks ran about, carrying beautiful cakes and goblets of rosy wine. The gnomes did ample justice to the fare. The children enjoyed it exceedingly, although the bites and sups were very small. The dwarfs then climbed the Christmas-tree and threw the fruit to the ladies. This caused much merriment. The children had their share, and when they could eat no more the King made them fill all their pockets.

At length, being tired, they wished to return home.

"Yes," said the King, "it is time you departed, for at midnight we return to our home beneath the earth. See, our sun grows pale; it bids us part. Yet first take these in memory of our feast." And he handed each child a pretty, covered basket. "There are little presents inside," he said, smiling; "use them well, and they will bring you happiness all your life long."

Paler and paler grew the sun. The musicians departed, playing a sad and plaintive melody. The children would have liked to open their baskets, but politeness forbade.

Instead, they thanked the King for his kindness, wished him good-night, and were led by him from the castle.

As they crossed the threshold their father stepped from behind the trees. He had waited there the whole time, and tried on all sides to enter the castle, but in vain. His anxiety had grown intense, and he rejoiced

" HE HANDED EACH CHILD A PRETTY, COVERED BASKET."

to see them return in safety. Taking the two youngest children in his arms, he hastened home, followed by the others.

On their way they told of all the music and splendour, and their father marvelled, for he had heard no music and seen no light. To his eyes the castle and the forest trees were black and gloomy as heretofore. But thus it is ever. The older folk gaze into the world with troubled eyes, and thus see only darkness and gloom, where to the children's eyes all is light, happiness, and joy.

In the baskets a fresh surprise awaited them. They contained neither gold nor precious stones, only pretty little tools, dainty, and bright as playthings. George and Paul each received every requisite for a shoemaker's trade. John and Karl a tailor's scissors, needle, and thimble. Katie and Christel had each a spinning-wheel.

The children laughed at the droll little presents, but their parents understood the deeper meaning that lay hidden beneath the apparent pleasantry, for they knew that the gnome is a friend to the industrious worker, and makes his work to prosper.

Years passed. A stately mansion with cowshed and pigsty replaced the shoemaker's cottage. Andrew and his wife were the richest people in the village.

This they owed to their children's industry or rather to the gnome's presents, for the brothers and sisters always used the tools the King had given them. George and Paul were celebrated shoemakers, and did work enough for four; John and Karl were first class tailors; whilst Katie and Christel were famed throughout the land for their beautiful spinning.

The villagers said Andrew must have found a treasure whilst taking his Christmas-tree to market; but the shoemaker and his family knew better, and when seated in their new mansion they often spoke with grateful remembrance of the "Gnome's Christmas Feast."

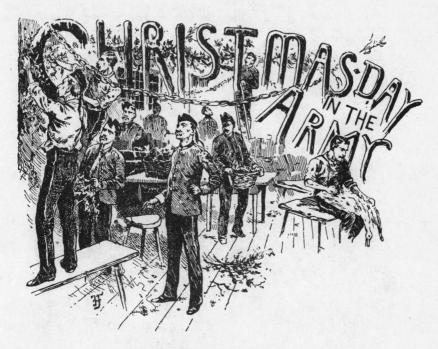

CHRISTMAS·DAY IN THE ARMY

By Horace Wyndham.

HE "General Return of the British Army" tells its readers that 222,373 non-commissioned officers and men comprise the effective strength of the Regular forces at the present moment. No statistics, however, are obtainable from which one can accurately ascertain the number of families in the United Kingdom which have one or more of their members privileged to wear the Queen's scarlet. Nevertheless, it may be safely asserted that there are very few English households indeed that have no connection with the Service. Under these circumstances, the immense amount of interest that is ever centred round the Army is perfectly natural. Unfortunately, the supply of information respecting the soldier's calling is severely limited, for, save when engaged on active service, the man in red is but little heard of.

It is a pity that this should be the case, for even in piping—or, rather, pipeclaying—times of peace, the daily round of duty in barracks is full of interest. Every season of the year has its own special work for the soldier, and the present one of winter is no exception. Foremost among the host of duties that now claim his attention is—according to his own views on the subject—the highly important one of preparing for Christmas. As the 25th of December only occurs once in twelve months, he naturally endeavours to make the most of it when it does come, and with this intention strains every nerve to make the day pass off successfully. His praiseworthy efforts in this direction are, it is pleasing to be able to record, ably seconded by his superiors. Thus, at Christmas time the commissioned ranks unbend to a marked extent, and the most cordial relations exist between all grades for these few hours. The reins of discipline are temporarily relaxed, and there is a general air of "standing at ease" that makes the day of special mark to the wearers of the Queen's scarlet wherever they may be stationed.

The Christmas festival throughout the Army is observed in a manner that is extremely characteristic of the British soldier. This is that of thoroughness. Nothing that is in the least degree slipshod is permitted to pass muster in connection with the day's routine. As a matter of fact, the 25th of

Spartan-like diet upon which the soldier is usually sustained is now replaced by a generous menu of turkey, beef, ham, plum-pudding, fruit, and practically unlimited beer. For the supply of all these good things the soldier is largely dependent upon the state of the canteen exchequer of his battalion. That is to say that, according to the amount of profit earned by this institution during the year, so will pecuniary grants be made therefrom at Christmas time for the purpose of purchasing seasonable fare. Then

PREPARATIONS IN THE COOK-HOUSE.

December is approached in a spirit that is almost akin to solemnity, and upon those charged with the direction of the different preparations for its due observance a heavy weight of responsibility rests. Upon their discharge of their duties depends the success or failure of the day.

The proverbial connection between Christmas and good cheer is in the Army observed to the letter, and a large quantity of refreshments—both solid and liquid—has, accordingly, to be procured. This is by reason of the fact that, on this eventful day, the rather

the commissioned ranks usually come forward as well and subscribe liberally towards the same purpose. It often happens, too, that officers who own preserves give orders for a present of game to be sent to the men of their companies just now. Then, after the solids have been thus arranged for, attention is devoted to the liquids which are necessary for washing them down. These take the form of barrels of ale, stout, and porter—spirits being rigorously tabooed—a small quantity of wine, and an ample supply of mineral waters. All these are taken charge of by the colour-sergeants of each company, and kept by them under lock and key until dinner-time on the 25th. This, as may be imagined, is a highly necessary precaution.

Just as coming events cast their shadows beforehand, so will a visit to a barrack-room during the few days that precede the great festival make abundantly clear what season is at hand. Thus, groups of men will be seen sitting round the fireplace busily occupied in stoning raisins for the pudding, or divesting geese and turkeys of their feathers; others will be engaged in fashioning festoons of coloured paper and wreaths of holly for decorative purposes; and a third party will

perform their work out of sight of most observers.

At 6 a.m. the sounding of *réveille* on the barrack-square by the bugler of the quarter-guard officially intimates to all concerned that Christmas Day has at last arrived. Ere the last sound of the call has finally died away into the frosty air, the great pile of buildings that houses the six or seven hundred men occupying the barracks becomes a scene of activity. Lights twinkle from numerous windows, and scores of men pass rapidly along dimly illuminated passages, *en route* to the lavatories, where they hastily perform their necessary ablutions. These

CHURCH PARADE.

be making themselves useful as messengers between the cook-house and the men's quarters. It is because space is so limited in the former institution that a part of the preliminary culinary preparations have to be carried out in the barrack-room. The press of work, too, makes this extraneous assistance very welcome to the accredited *chefs*, who, like the stokers on a battleship,

completed, beds have to be neatly made up, floors swept, and rooms generally garnished.

There is no drill carried out to-day, for in the Army Sunday routine is observed on Christmas morning. Accordingly, as soon as breakfast is over, all hands set to work to smarten themselves up for church parade. The "fall-in" for this ceremony will probably be sounded at half-past ten. On account of the fact that a large number of men are enjoying a month's furlough just now, the number attending this parade is usually of rather attenuated proportions. However, there will probably be some 300 at any rate following the band to the garrison church. As soon as the building is reached and the troops are disposed of in the seats appropriated to their use, the chaplain commences the service.

This is not of any great duration, for, knowing his congregation as he does, the

have been busily employed in making active preparations for the dinner that is about to take place. For this purpose the barrack-room tables (which, in special honour of the day, are on this occasion covered with cloths) have been laid for the meal, the liquids brought in, and the rooms smartened up afresh. At twenty minutes to one the bugle peals out its welcome bidding : " *Come to the cook-house do-o-or, Boys !* " and away rush the orderlies to this important institution. Here they receive from the company cooks the dishes allotted to their respective messes

THE COLONEL'S INSPECTION.

military cleric wisely refrains from indulging in a long disquisition upon the purpose for which they are assembled. Instead of this, he delivers a brief, plainly expressed discourse that is productive of infinitely more good than would be a volume of sermons from the most eloquent members of the whole Episcopal Bench.

On the conclusion of the service the troops are marched back to barracks and dismissed to their own quarters. During their absence, the men detailed to act as "cooks' mates"

and carry them off to their rooms, where they are quickly carved by another batch of helpers. The dinners for the men on the quarter-guard are taken to them by the orderly-men, and similarly those for such others as are absent on picquet-duty are put aside.

On the stroke of one o'clock the hard-worked bugler sounds again, and everyone is now required to be sitting down in his place at the table. Five minutes later a business-like attack is being carried out upon the good cheer that loads the festive board. The junior N.C.O.'s act as waiters, and are kept busily employed in ministering to the lusty appetites of the diners. Imperative demands for "another yard of ham here," or "a pound or two off the turkey—with plenty of padding, corporal," arise on every side, and a cheerful popping of corks, mingling with a thirst-inspiring trickling from the

of the day, is going round the barracks. In a minute or two the party arrives at our typical room and is received by the colour-sergeant. The commanding officer expresses a hope that the men are enjoying their dinner, and turns to leave. This is the cue for the N.C.O.

"Beg your pardon, sir," he commences, with much confusion, "but the company

AFTER-DINNER SMOKING CONCERT.

beer-barrels, testifies abundantly to the appreciation with which their efforts are being met.

Suddenly the colour-sergeant, who is temporarily presiding, orders a cessation of hostilities and calls everyone to "attention." His quick ear has detected a clanking of swords and jingling of spurred heels in the corridor outside, and he knows that this heralds the approach of the colonel, who, accompanied by the adjutant and subaltern

would—er—like—that is—er—would be proud to drink your very good health, sir."

"Dear me," returns the colonel, blandly, simulating great surprise, "I'm extremely obliged, really."

"Sherry wine, or port, sir?" inquires the colour-sergeant, advancing towards him with two black bottles, and trying to recollect the respective liquors in each.

"Oh, whatever you like, colour-sergeant," returns the other, accommodatingly. "Not too much though," he adds, hastily, as a large glass of "sherry wine" is handed him.

"'A' Company—Attention!" commands the N.C.O., in his drill-parade voice. "I have much pleasure in proposing the health of our colonel. Private Jones, just keep your hands off that plum duff for half a minute."

"Here, here! For he's a jolly good fellow —Proper sort to make old Kruger sit up!" and various other complimentary epithets are promptly called forth by this address. When the applause has subsided somewhat, the colonel seizes his opportunity.

"Non-commissioned officers and men of 'A' Company," he remarks, "I am much gratified at the honour you have paid me. Glad to see you enjoying yourselves, and hope you will all spend a merry Christmas." Then he snatches up his sword, and, signalling to the other members of his party, promptly hurries off to the next company's block.

After the commanding officer has thus been toasted, a similar compliment is paid to the captain and subalterns who administer the affairs of the assembly. As precisely the same ceremony takes place in every barrack-room at this time, it can well be under-

stood that a good deal of toasting is got through.

At length, however, the colonel's tour is completed, and he retires to his own quarters. The other officers and the sergeants follow his example, and accordingly withdraw to their own messes, where they also celebrate the festive occasion in an appropriate, if rather different, manner. In the barrack-rooms the rank-and-file are now left to themselves for the remainder of the afternoon. This is generally spent in the carrying out of a smoking concert—for alcoholic refreshment always seems to incline the soldier's thoughts towards harmony. Accordingly, a temporary stage of forms and tables is hastily erected, and the budding Sims Reeves's among the revellers are called upon to display their vocal talents. Thus a couple of hours or so are agreeably passed, and, as long as any liquid remains in the beer-barrels, no one seems to think of seeking distraction elsewhere. By nightfall, however, the troops usually commence to change into "walking-out" dress, and soon the barracks are practically deserted. At 9.30 p.m. a roll-call takes place, and, three-quarters of an hour later, the sounding by the orderly bugler of "lights out" proclaims the official expiry of Christmas Day.

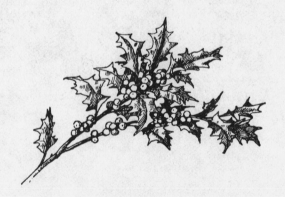

THE Lady's Realm

Xmas
Double Number

CONTRIBUTORS:

MARIE CORELLI
SARAH GRAND
M. E. BRADDON
FRANKFORT MOORE
S. BARING-GOULD
COUNTESS OF CORK
LADY G. RAMSDEN
HON. AGNES LEIGH
EDNA LYALL
H.E. LADY CURRIE
SIR EDWIN ARNOLD
ELLA MACMAHON

1s

HARE'S CHROMOTYPE.

No. 14.   Vol. 3.

DECEMBER.

150 ILLUSTRATIONS.

PORTRAITS AND AUTOGRAPHS.

CHRISTMAS PRESENTS.

IT would certainly be difficult to find a more welcome gift than some trifle bought at the Parisian Diamond Company's, 143, Regent Street, W.; 85, New Bond Street, W.; and 43, Burlington Arcade, W. The beautiful designs of this firm are well known, and at the Victorian Era Exhibition a gold medal was awarded them for their "Orient" pearls and perfection in diamond-mounting and setting. This firm was awarded a gold medal at the Paris Exhibition in 1889, but it is particularly gratifying to know that English people are at last learning to appreciate the art of designing.

As space is limited, I must only specify a few of the fascinating novelties to be obtained here.

Perhaps first and foremost we should take hair-ornaments. These play a very important part in Paris fashions at the present moment, and it is probable they will find equal favour

From the Parisian Diamond Co.

in London. No woman can be well dressed nowadays unless her head is *bien garni* as well as *bien coiffé*. One of the lightest and most elegant designs I have ever beheld was a comb with three diamond fuchsias springing from a leaf, the petals of which shook as the wearer moved.

There are combs of various shapes for the back, the front, and the sides of the head. The majority of those worn across the back are wide and of a beautiful scroll pattern. A heavier comb was composed of two rows of diamonds, surmounted with five big pearls springing from a network of leaves. This was particularly pretty for the back of the head; but it could be turned round and worn on the fringe in the form of a tiara.

Very inexpensive was a double clasp to be worn on a velvet ribbon for the neck, or else as a buckle to clasp some old lace on a Russian sable muff. A lovely pendant or brooch had one large pearl in the centre, with hanging festoons of diamonds, from which fell a drop pearl. A delicate design in ivy-leaves, with a trefoil in pearls surrounded by small brilliants, could be worn as a spray or screwed on to a comb and used as a hair-ornament. For a classical head what could be prettier than a band of diamonds, only to be described as the Marquise Bandeau, that, when

the hair is worn low, is wound round the coils at the back?

There are buckles galore, and we cannot exist without a Louis XVI. buckle in these days, any more than we can live without a "dangle" of sorts. Some of the most delightful of these latter are the little diamond lucky pigs, with ruby eyes and curly tails, frogs in diamonds and emeralds, stars and trefoils. Many of these attractions come within the range of the purses of everybody wishing to be generous at Christmastide.

A more costly present would be a pearl festoon necklace, with three little oyster-shells of diamonds, each set with a pearl in the centre as a drop pearl. In this we see a specimen of the celebrated "Orient" pearls that defy detection. I may add that the necklace was one of the most becoming and graceful that I have ever seen. Would that space permitted me to descant on the beautiful corsage pieces in Louis XV. and Louis XVI. designs that are sold by the Parisian Diamond Company!

"A PRESENT TO CHEER."

A DELIGHTFUL and inexpensive novelty is the musical box known as "The Polyphon," which has gained distinct popularity. It is of foreign manufacture, and can be had from Nicole Frères, 21, Ely Place, London, E.C. It plays a thousand tunes, and sounds a ridiculously cheap toy at 16s. 6d. This is a case where one indeed feels that there is a great deal to be had for the money.

ATTRACTIVE SOUVENIRS FOR CHRISTMAS AT THE 4711 DEPÔT.

NOTHING can be more acceptable as a Christmas present than a bottle containing one of the perfumes distilled by the 4711 Depôt, of 62, New Bond Street, W. Perhaps one of the favourite scents of the day is Mülhen's Rhine Violet. I advise my readers, when buying this, which is, of course, sold by all respectable chemists and perfumers, to be sure and ask for "*Mülhen's*," or they may be put off with some inferior Rhine Violet. Imitation, they say, is the sincerest form of flattery, yet I am sure that the 4711 Depôt would thankfully dispense with such esteem, for they have naturally suffered much by their customers obtaining a worthless imitation of the genuine article. This firm have lately brought out the Rhine Violet in the natural colour; the delightful odour is in no way impaired by this process, as no chemicals are used in producing it.

Any perfume emanating from the 4711 Depôt, such as the Lily of the Valley, Malmaison, White Rose, White Lilac, Jessamine, Ylang Ylang, etc., may be had in all kinds of inexpensive and tasteful cut-glass bottles, embedded in satin and tied with ribbons. These may be bought from 3s. 6d. upwards, and would indeed make an ideal *cadeau*.

Very delightful are the salts in various shades and perfumes. A great favourite is the Eau-de-Cologne Salts in a purse, for travelling purposes, sold at the modest price of 1s. 9d. But who, nowadays, does not wish to have her soap perfumed with the scent she uses? No more welcome gift could be had than a box of fancy soaps. Particularly delicious are the Lilac, Violet, Heliotrope, Lily of the Valley, New Mown Hay, etc.

Christmas Presents.

There is also a goodly collection of silver-topped perfume and salts-bottles, and powder-boxes in all shapes. One cannot go far wrong in choosing as a present a bottle of Mülhen's 4711 perfumes. A new catalogue of the same has now been issued and can be obtained post free on application.

AT THE ALADDIN PALACE OF LAMPS.

HERE indeed do dainty presents meet the eye on every side. I think first and foremost the white china table ornaments especially appeal to us, and particularly those used for lighting purposes. They are made of the finest white Stafford, and the designs are most beautiful and original. Here, too, is to be seen every kind of lamp and candle, and every sort of shade.

For the dining-table nothing could be nicer than the white china flower-stands, fitted with candle-holders; these candles deserve particular mention, as they are non-smouldering and non-guttering; they are known as the Molucca's candle. To complete the table decoration we see shades in different-coloured accordion-pleated flowered gauze, with white china menu-stands.

On the subject of lamps and candle-shades as seen at 92, New Bond Street, I could write volumes. Particularly pretty are those representing flowers, such as tulips, lilies, etc. The larger shades are generally in *mousseline-de-soie* or silk of two colours. Any of the shades, apart from the stands, candles, or lamps, themselves, would make extremely nice presents. A visit to the Aladdin Palace of Lamps does indeed admit one to Wonderland.

AT THE ARCTIC LAMP COMPANY'S.

A THOROUGHLY excellent invention, and one, too, as charming as it is excellent. I refer now to the "Arctic lamp," a delightful little illumination which Messrs. Green, Brothers, brought out a season or two ago, which they now offer in a perfected form.

What is the "Arctic Lamp"? It may be described as a candle-holder, constructed somewhat on the same

principle as the old carriage-lamp. To be a little more explicit, the lamp consists of a tube, in white or a variety of delicate shades, in which the candle is enclosed, and pushed up as it is burnt by means of a spiral spring inside. By this means, not a scrap of the candle is wasted; the ugly guttering, too, that so spoils the appearance of such a light, is quite done away with, while it can be extinguished immediately without any unpleasant odour remaining. The advantages of the "Arctic Lamp" in place of the ordinary candle must be obvious to every one. A great point is their safety, as, being unaffected by draught, they burn perfectly steadily. The next great point is their charming appearance when lit, and the ease with which they can be fitted to any kind of bracket.

From the Arctic Lamp Company.

Messrs. Green Brothers have been very wise in this way, and now offer to the public an immense choice of stands and holders for their clever invention; and these can be bought together, or separately, complete with charming shades,

I can suggest nothing prettier for a Christmas gift than a pair of fitted Arctic lamps. For dinner-table decoration they are quite unrivalled. For the present season I would suggest the attention of my readers being given to the lamp fitted into a delightfully patterned gilt or silver stand, and with a quaint silk shade, edged with a heavy silk fringe to match. Then my heart goes out to some perfectly sweet flower-holders in enamelled metal, in the shape of troughs, which must be filled with blossoms or ferns, from which the lamp rises, crowned with a dainty silk shade in any colour liked. Nor are these expensive, being sold at 8s. 6d. each. The utility of this invention should commend it perhaps more strongly than anything else to our notice. For reading, sewing, playing the piano, an "Arctic Lamp" is not to be beaten, as it gives a soft, steady, clear light, with three times the force of an ordinary candle. While, on the practical side, I may say that the lamps can be fitted to any candlestick, as they are made with adjustable spring-ends, or with these in rubber. Their price per pair varies from 8s. to 11s. 6d. It must be remembered that the lamp, once bought, will last a lifetime, and is therefore an investment of true economy.

From the Arctic Lamp Company.

Those of my readers who can should pay a visit to 179, Regent Street, W., where they will see this charming idea in working order, and be also able to glance through the lovely collection of holders, stands, shades, etc , which go to complete the lamp and make it an ideal table decoration.

AT MESSRS. STOCKLEY & SONS'.

AND now, what could I more fittingly go to than the delightful subject of table accessories, to be found at Messrs. Stockley & Sons' quite unique little establishment in New Bond Street.

Mr. Stockley certainly has gained the reputation of having quite the smartest and prettiest wares in London. Any new idea is seized by him with avidity, and his own inventive brain has been responsible for bringing out some of the most delightful novelties of the season. One of the most charming, which will certainly go well, is a *soufflé* case, this being composed of tissue paper in a delicate shade of green, most cleverly twisted and plaited to resemble basketwork,

From Messrs. Stockley & Sons.

and then finished with a full frill of a contrasting colour and little twisted handle, tied with a tiny bow of ribbon, to match. The ones I liked best had frills of mauve, and looked quite lovely in a mauve and

149

pink table decoration. The idea is Mr. Stockley's own, and the cases can only be had from his establishment.

Candle-shades are another specialty here, and I give an illustration of a model that is running very strongly. This consists of double frills of delicate-hued silk, like the petals of a flower tied round with ribbons. Mr. Stockley's menu-cards are quite famous for originality of design, and the same may be said of his stationery, in which he indeed sets the fashion. The fancy note-paper of the moment is in a pale shade of dove-grey, with a tiny stamped edge of white, the envelopes being long and narrow, or very broad. This must be termed an ideal establishment for Christmas gifts, and my readers cannot do better than pay a speedy visit there, for Mr. Stockley can show them a hundred knick-knacks to delight a recipient.

WHIFFS FROM THE SOUTH OF FRANCE.

WHAT more acceptable gift in dreary December in England could be imagined than a veritable whiff from the south of France, in the form of a bottle of H. P. Truefitt's well-known White or Purple Lilac?

From H. P. Truefitt, 13 and 14, Old Bond Street; and Burlington Arcade.

Nothing is more delicious, no scent more pungent, and really indistinguishable from the flower itself. Perhaps the purple makes the prettier present, for it is in a glorious shade—which does not, however, stain the handkerchief. As the illustration shows, one bottle, in a box lined with satin of the same colour, tied with ribbon, may be had as low as 6s. (Of course, there are soaps and sachet-powders to be had to correspond.) A huge bottle of this scent, in a beautiful box, is really cheap at a guinea.

There is also a variety of cut-glass sprays and bottles suitable for Christmas presents, which can be filled with any perfume. Cut-glass, silver-mounted sprays, are obtainable from 3s. 6d. upwards, and cut-glass salts-bottles, in all shades from 2s. 6d.

A glance in the window at the Burlington Arcade Entrance will show a trayful of lovely knick-knacks in amber tortoiseshell. Amongst the hair-ornaments some are quite plain, showing all the new shapes and designs; other are mounted with paste. Hair-brushes in real ivory, ebony boxes, cut-glass bottles,

silver cases, fancy fans, silver curling-tongs and lamps, triple mirrors, etc., are but a few of the delightful novelties to be seen at 13 and 14, Old Bond Street, W.

To return to perfumes. The Imperial Bouquet was brought out for the Jubilee, and is composed of spicy essences from the woods of Australia and India. The "Record" perfume is another souvenir of the Jubilee, made by Truefitt. Always popular are the well-known Violette de Parme, and the Bouquet Cecil.

A suitable present for a man is their Lavender Water, twenty years old, double distilled and sold in quaint old English bottles. It is a recognised fact that the one scent a man is not ashamed to use is Lavender. This essence is indeed worthy of a trial.

I FORESEE how "all the World and his Wife" will flock to Messrs. Maple's in a few days' time, for is not this giant establishment crammed with fascinating novelties, which absolutely tear the money from one's purse, and cry to be bought?

Out of all, I fixed my attention on china and clocks, thinking that either or both form suitable Yule-tide offerings. The only difficulty which arises is that there is too much choice. For instance, my first love went out entirely to the delightful pieces of Worcester which I noted here. For beauty of design and colouring it would be quite impossible to find their rival, and I consider that Messrs. Maple are to be congratulated on such a unique collection. The modern "delft" comes next, and this has ever been one of my favourites in its antique form. The reproductions here satisfy even my critical soul—and indeed, it would take an expert to tell them from the original. The delightfully moderate price at which each piece was marked struck me particularly; a delicious little bit could be bought for three shillings, this being the quaintest *sabot*, to be used as a flower-holder. Then there are bowls, jars, plates and dishes, of every size and shape, and for those who possess an oaken dining-room, nothing could be more acceptable than a bit of blue delft. I was charmed also with the Dutch ware here, this is so quaint and distinctive—and indeed, there are ornaments of every country, from Holland to Japan.

Another specialty, however, which personally I am much attached to is the beautiful Damascus work, of which Messrs. Maple have a unique collection. This, too, is wonderfully cheap, and a pair of charming pots, to be used as fern-holders, can be bought for the modest 5s. The English brass-work in this department is worth notice too; a remarkably handsome pot, to hold a giant palm, can be bought for a guinea. From here I wandered into the clock department. For these fascinating articles I have a deep affection, and my taste Messrs. Maple gratify to the fullest extent, for they offer me clocks of every shape, size, and design, from the stately silver-chimed grandfather to the tiniest little gem of a timepiece which marked the flight of the hours in the days of Louis XV. Those entitled carriage-clocks in pretty brass cases at 18s. 9d. are great bargains, and a screen clock at 20s. also struck me as worthy of notice. There are some exquisite specimens of gilt and enamel, all of which are faithful copies of old designs, and, as wedding and birthday gifts, would prove ideal; but indeed, it is impossible in such a short notice to catalogue one tithe of the novelties in these departments. Suffice to say that all that is beautiful, as well as all that is useful, is to be found at Messrs. Maple's, and the steps of those intent on Christmas gift purchases cannot be better directed than to this wonderful establishment in the Tottenham Court Road.

THE CUISINE

Mary A SIBREE

BY MRS. DE SALIS.

SHOP windows are full of Christmas cards and Christmas presents, heralding that Yule-tide is very near. Young people are counting the days to their holidays, conjuring up visions of theatres and Christmas dances. We will now try to give amongst our recipes one or two for juvenile parties.

Celery Sandwiches.

Grate some celery very fine till it makes about three tablespoonfuls; put it in a basin, add a little salt, and mix in a small pot of Devonshire cream to a thick paste. Butter some slices of Hovis bread and spread it with the celery cream, place another buttered slice on the top, then stamp out into rounds. Decorate with some of the green celery leaves.

Nouveauté Sandwiches.

Cut up some cold turkey, pass it through a mincing machine with a quarter the quantity of ham and a dozen oysters; pound together in the mortar; mix in some velouté sauce, with salt and pepper to taste, and pass through a fine sieve. Spread this mixture on bread and butter, and make into sandwiches. A slice of aspic jelly placed inside each sandwich makes a still better relish.

Chicken à l'Andalouse.

(Luncheon Dish.)

Cut up a fowl into joints; fry a couple of chopped carrots and four onions in butter, and, when brown, add the joints of fowl; season with pepper, salt, and a little paprika, and toss over the fire for ten or twelve minutes. Make a sauce with a tablespoonful of flour, half a pint of stock made from the carcase of the chicken, a wine-glass of chablis, a small piece of lemon thyme, and three tomatoes skinned and seeded; cook this, and stir it into the sautépan with the chicken and vegetables, and cook for half an hour. Now add half a dozen chopped mushrooms, and leave on the fire for another ten minutes; then dish up the pieces of chicken prettily, and pour the sauce and vegetables over, and sprinkle with chopped parsley.

Raised Woodcock Pie.

Bone a couple of woodcocks, cook them, then cut them in two. Make a good forcemeat with veal and some poultry livers and the trails of the woodcock, which two latter have been fried; season well, then put it in a mortar with some cooked ham fat. Put the bones and forcemeat into a saucepan with two shallots and a sprig of thyme, and cover them with stock to make a good gravy. Line a pie-mould with pastry; arrange some of the forcemeat at the bottom, and line the sides with it, then place one of the woodcocks; cover with two or three sliced truffles and another layer of forcemeat; place the remaining woodcock on the top of this, then more truffles, and another layer of forcemeat; when full, mask the top with slices of bacon. Cover the pie, set the pie-dish in a sautépan, with a glass of hot water, and bake it in a moderate oven for an hour and a half. Half an hour after it has been taken from the oven, pour into it some of the gravy made from the bones, in which three sheets of gelatine should have been dissolved. To be served cold.

Neapolitan Cream.

Put half an ounce of the best gelatine into a small saucepan, with a quarter of a pint of cold water, to soak; then place it on the fire and stir till the gelatine is melted; add two ounces of castor sugar. Whip to a stiff froth half a pint of double cream, and stir in the gelatine through a strainer; divide the cream into five parts and place in five basins. Mix a tablespoonful of made coffee into one, a tablespoonful of maraschino liqueur into a second, two tablespoonfuls of pounded pistachios coloured with a little sap green colouring into the third, two tablespoonfuls of strawberry jam passed through a sieve, coloured with a little cochineal, into the fourth, and into the fifth two tablespoonfuls of apricot jam passed through a sieve and coloured with a little saffron yellow. Have a Neapolitan mould ready, or, if one is not handy, use a plain round mould, and put a layer of lemon jelly, coloured red, at the bottom; and when set, add, one at a time, the different creams in layers, waiting till each is set before putting in another. Arrange the colours tastily, and this makes, not only a very delicious, but a very pretty dish. Put on ice for two hours, and turn out. Garnish with sugar violets and glacé cherries.

Apple Hedgehog.

Take twenty-four small apples, peel and core them. Make a syrup with a quarter of a pound of sugar and a quarter of a pint of water. When the sugar is melted, add the apples, and stew them till quite soft. Mash them, and then lay them in a compote dish, and pile them up in a pyramid. Whip up half a pint of double cream, flavour with vanilla, and pour over thickly; strew with chopped almonds and pistachio kernels.

GLORY TO GOD

A VERY
HAPPY
CHRISTMAS
TO YOU!

IN THE HIGHEST